I0821258

52 PRAYERS FOR MY HUSBAND

A Tyndale nonfiction imprint

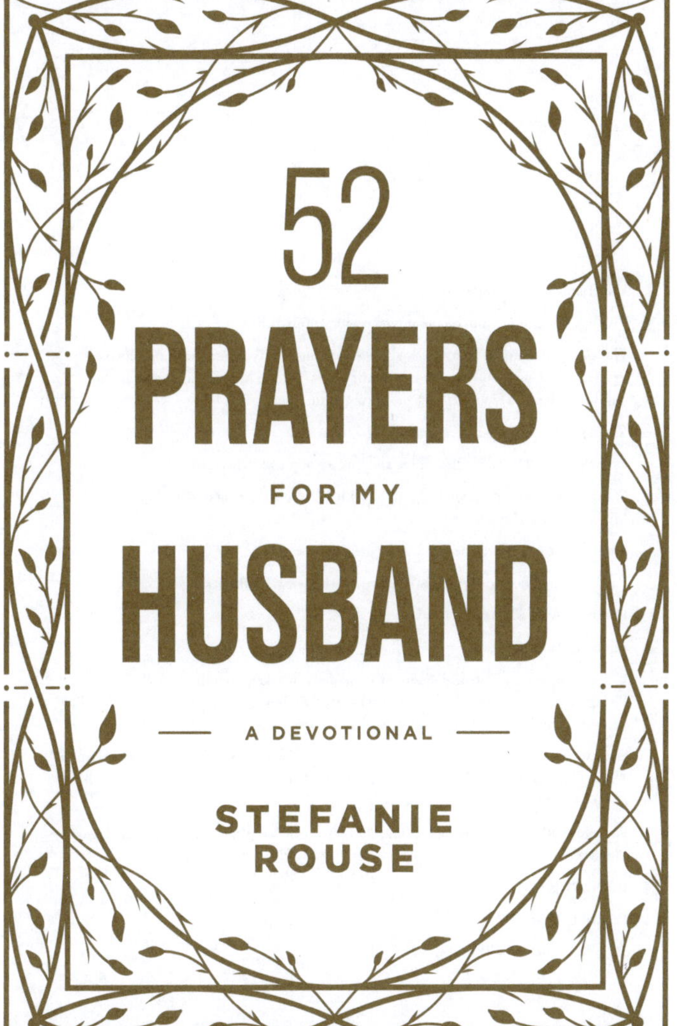

52 PRAYERS FOR MY HUSBAND

A DEVOTIONAL

STEFANIE ROUSE

Visit Tyndale online at tyndale.com.

Visit Tyndale Momentum online at tyndalemomentum.com.

Tyndale, Tyndale's quill logo, *Tyndale Momentum,* and the Tyndale Momentum logo are registered trademarks of Tyndale House Ministries. Tyndale Momentum is a nonfiction imprint of Tyndale House Publishers, Carol Stream, Illinois.

52 Prayers for My Husband: A Devotional

Published in association with The Bindery Agency, www.TheBinderyAgency.com.

Designed by Sarah Susan Richardson

Edited by Donna L. Berg

For information about special discounts for bulk purchases, please contact Tyndale House Publishers at csresponse@tyndale.com, or call 1-855-277-9400.

ISBN 979-8-4005-0104-3

Printed in China

30 29 28 27 26 25 24
7 6 5 4 3 2 1

To Caleb, the champion of my heart,

your eyes hold the story of our love, from the first spark to the enduring flame. In them, I see the incredible man God made you to be—full of humility, kindness, and unwavering love. I feel God's love through you. Your eyes have been an anchor through every joy and trial, filling me with peace from Christ and deepening our connection with each glance. This book is a tribute to the love that shines in your eyes and the way you illuminate my world with your presence. Thank you for looking at me with so much love and for believing in me and being my best friend and the love of my life.

And to every wife reading these words,

may your journey be blessed with love, healing, and a renewed appreciation for the gift of your husband. As you water the seeds of your marriage with prayer and love, may God's grace flourish in your relationship, bringing forth beauty and strength. Embrace each moment with gratitude. May this book inspire you to be the best wife you can be, knowing that God walks with you every step of the way.

Introduction

Dear beloved reader,

My husband, Caleb, and I have sought to keep prayer as the foundation of our relationship. There are times when neither of us has anything left in our love tank, but God sustains us. We've seen the power of prayer and the amazing way He has transformed our lives and relationship. He's helped us and been with us through the best times and the hardest times.

As a wife, I've had times when I've tried to fix my husband myself. When I try to take too much control (I can sometimes still do this), I hinder God's work. As I keep learning to surrender my husband to God, and look to see the best in him, my marriage and life thrive so much more. I believe that your marriage, too, can become even more beautiful over time as you pour your energies into prayer for your husband.

I am thrilled to embark on this journey of spiritual and marital growth with you. As a Christian relationship coach with a passion for nurturing marriages, I've created this guide to help you strengthen the bond between yourself and your husband through the power of prayer and purposeful action. My hope is that we as wives can grow to be more like Jesus through this journey—to be women who increasingly honor, respect, and love our husbands.

Marriage is a beautiful gift from God, but it requires intentional effort and continuous nourishment to thrive. Prayer is a dynamic force that can transform both *your* heart and your husband's heart, leading to a more fulfilling and God-centered marriage. Prayer is not just a passive request but a powerful tool for transformation. As you pray, you invite God to work within you and your marriage, aligning your desires with His will. With purposeful prayer, you can watch your relationship grow stronger and healthier, knowing that you are partnering with the Creator of love and marriage.[1]

This devotional is designed to be a weekly companion for your journey. For each week, you'll find a specific topic for prayer and reflection, including your husband's spiritual growth, his physical and emotional well-being, his relationship with you, and his relationships with others.

At the top of the page, you'll find Scripture that goes along with the topic. Memorizing or meditating on these verses each week is a helpful way to remind yourself of God's truth that trumps our emotions and circumstances.

Next, I'll share a personal story of how prayer has played a role in my own marriage as we've dealt with the particular topic. I'm sure that many of the issues we've struggled with will sound familiar to you. I hope it will encourage you to know that these are common to many marriages. After my story, you'll find a suggested prayer for the topic, helping you to pray specifically, intentionally, and with purpose for the daily needs of your spouse.

You will also find a summarizing word of encouragement intended to help you keep the topic at the front of your mind throughout the week. You might want to write it on a sticky note to remind yourself to put it into practice every day.

In addition to prayer, I've included practical "Love in Action" suggestions for each week, which are designed to help you apply the principles discussed in each devotional. These calls to action begin

---

1 You might also be interested in our companion book, *52 Prayers for My Wife: A Devotional*, written by my husband, Caleb, in case you and your husband would like to join efforts on this journey.

with one special activity you can do together with your husband. However, I understand that every marriage is unique, and in case your husband seems resistant or uninterested, I've also included a second activity that you can do on his behalf, which does not require his participation. The goal is to invest in your marriage and demonstrate love in tangible ways. In any case, be sure your husband knows you are praying for him regularly. I'm sure it will be a huge encouragement to him.

It is my hope that this approach allows you to immerse yourself fully in the topic, providing time for you to pray earnestly for your husband to flourish in various aspects of life, as well as for you to grow as a wife as you seek to support him.

I encourage you to embrace this prayer guide with an open heart, knowing that growth takes time and patience. Each devotional is an opportunity to deepen your connection with God and your husband. It's an invitation to seek God's wisdom, guidance, and blessings for your marriage.

I want to walk alongside you on this journey. I believe in the power of prayer and the potential for transformation within your marriage. It is my sincere hope that this guide will inspire you, uplift your spirit, and breathe new life into your relationship.

May your journey through this guide be filled with love, grace, and the presence of God. May your marriage be a testament to His goodness and faithfulness. Together, let's nurture the love that God has planted in your heart and watch it flourish as you commit to a year of prayerful growth.

With love and blessings,

Stefanie Rouse
Christian relationship coach

WEEK

1

CALLING FORTH THE GOOD

A prayer that he would walk in his God-given purpose

Don't copy the behavior and customs of this world, but let God transform you into a new person by changing the way you think. Then you will learn to know God's will for you, which is good and pleasing and perfect.

ROMANS 12:2

When I first met Caleb, I was captivated by his kindness, passion for God, and zest for life. His unwavering commitment to Christ and boldness in sharing the love of Jesus are still an inspiration.

During the initial years of our marriage, I observed Caleb's remarkable ability to impact his students. His classroom was a sanctuary of love and encouragement, and even the "outcast" kids felt so welcomed and loved. I kept calling forth these qualities in my husband, and it encouraged him to step out even more into his God-given purpose.

I also admired Caleb's boldness in taking on new opportunities, whether it was speaking in front of a crowd or sharing his faith with someone on the street. As we ventured into entrepreneurship and ministry, Caleb embraced further challenges, such as creating videos for social media. I felt overwhelmed, but he remained undeterred.

As a result, millions around the world have been touched by the gospel, and Christlike relationships have begun to flourish. Caleb's unwavering faith allowed God to work wonders.

God has a special purpose for your husband, too, and He has given him spiritual gifts along with his own unique way to use them. Encouraging your husband and going along with his ideas that honor God (even if they're scary) can be such a blessing to your marriage and God's Kingdom.

Heavenly Father, I thank You for the gift of my husband. *You know his heart, his struggles, his aspirations. I pray that he walks in the purpose You have uniquely designed for him. May he find his identity deeply rooted in You, standing strong as a man after Your own heart. Fill him with courage, wisdom, and discernment each day. Help him not to try to fit in with the world but to go to You for his sense of worth.*

Lord, help me to love like You love. I pray that I can be a wife who uplifts, supports, and honors her husband in all seasons of life. Teach me to also love You more deeply, so that my love for him is an extension of Your love. May I be a vessel of Your grace, kindness, and encouragement in his life. Let my worth come from You first and foremost, so I can love him out of the overflow.

I pray for our marriage to be so deeply rooted in Christ that others are led to discover their identity in You. Let us walk boldly in the unique way You've made us, encouraging each other always. In the powerful and life-changing name of Jesus, I pray. Amen.

Boldly walking in the purpose God has for us can lead to incredible blessings and opportunities.

love in action . . .

Together: Talk about ways you see God has gifted the other person. Pray about how to use these gifts for the Kingdom.

For him: Tell your husband ways you see qualities in his life making a positive impact in God's Kingdom.

WEEK

2

DEALING WITH WOUNDS

A prayer for healing from current or past pain

He heals the brokenhearted and binds up their wounds.

PSALM 147:3, NIV

"I've never told anyone this before, but I felt I needed to tell you," Caleb said.

We had only been dating a few months, but we both felt more at home with each other than we'd ever felt before. I held both of his hands tight as he talked. It was hard to fathom. How could this horrible thing have happened to my precious Caleb when he was young?

This violation of love and trust had wounded him deeply. Asking God silently for strength, I hugged Caleb and assured him it wasn't his fault. I cried with him and told him how I wished I could have protected him. Caleb felt such freedom and safety in being seen in this area of pain he had kept hidden for years. It has been such an honor to walk with him, with Jesus beside us, and see the wounds heal.

All these years later, I still have a strong desire to be an advocate for healing over my husband's wounds. Sometimes I'm great at this. At other times, I've made the wounds worse out of my own places of pain. But Jesus is the Mighty Counselor and Great Physician. I keep running to God, and He pours out more love to me so I can extend that compassion to my beloved.

Heavenly Father, I lift up my husband to You today. *Heal the scars and wounds from his past—whether physical, emotional, or relational. Let Your presence reach any pain, insecurities, or fears he may carry. Transform these broken pieces into testimonies of Your power and love. Help me to be an advocate of healing to him. Teach me when to speak, when to hug, when to kiss, and when to remain silent. Let me trust You, Lord, to be the Great Healer for him.*

God, mend the wounds and scars from my own past that can hinder me from loving my husband fully. Transform my pain into wisdom and my brokenness into compassion, so that I can love him not out of my wounds but out of Your wholeness. Help me to love You first and most, for only then can I love my husband as he deserves.

Let us not hold each other's histories against one another, but rather see each other through Your eyes—redeemed, loved, and new creations in Christ. May this grace free us from resentment or judgment, allowing for a marriage that radiates Your unconditional love and forgiveness to others.

I pray, Father, that the healing we experience individually and as a couple would lay the foundation for a marriage deeply rooted in Christ. Amen.

God is the Great Physician, and He wants to heal us physically, mentally, emotionally, and spiritually.

love in action . . .

Together: Create a "Grace Jar" for recording moments when one of you shows grace, especially toward past wounds. Read the items together.

For him: Identify wounds that might affect your ability to love your husband fully. Hand them to God for His healing touch.

WEEK

3

UNLOCKING HIS HEART

A prayer that your husband will feel appreciated

Fix your thoughts on what is true, and honorable, and right, and pure, and lovely, and admirable. Think about things that are excellent and worthy of praise.

PHILIPPIANS 4:8

"Kitchen 101, Caleb," I said with a snarky tone. I had just bumped my hip on the pan handle he had left sticking out from the stovetop in our small galley kitchen. I could instantly see the shame on his face, and I wished I could shove the words back into my mouth.

Caleb had excitedly offered to cook dinner after a hard day at work. But instead of thanking him, the first thing I mentioned was a correction. This is the very opposite of how to unlock a man's heart.

Our husbands' love and feelings of connection to us are unlocked when they feel respected and appreciated. Although we can't always take back our words, we can strive to do better moving forward.

"Caleb, thank you for the huge sacrifice and love of cooking for our family. I love and appreciate you so much." How much differently our interaction could have gone if I had said this instead! Our words and our nonverbal expressions of gratitude go a long way. As I overlook small, negative things and spend more time pointing out the good, holy, excellent, praiseworthy things I see in my husband, my marriage thrives.

Dear God, thank You for the most special man to share this life with! *What a gift he is! My husband is so beautifully created as Your masterpiece. Thank You for the wonderful and unique way You've made him—the way he laughs, the sound of his voice, his scent, the way he kisses me. I'm so grateful for this precious soul You've entrusted to me to love and care for, and I pray that he will always feel loved and appreciated.*

Lord, I desire to be a grateful wife. Help me always to see the best in my husband. Let me assume the best about him. Help me to point out the good things and close my mouth if something unkind or critical is about to come out. For the times I've been ungrateful in the past, will You heal my husband's heart and help me walk in a new path of thankfulness?

Holy Spirit, let no root of bitterness grow in our marriage, but rather one of love, patience, kindness, goodness, gentleness, and self-control. May the gratitude cultivated in our marriage spread a fragrant blessing to those we encounter each day, pointing them to Your love. Amen.

The more I tell my husband how much I appreciate him, the more I will see reasons to show him my gratitude.

love in action . . .

Together: Start a new practice of naming three specific things each day that you are grateful for in the other person.

For him: On sticky notes, write ways your husband brightens your day. Place them around the house where he will see them.

WEEK

4

I ONLY HAVE EYES FOR YOU

A prayer for purity in your marriage

Drink water from your own well—share your love only with your wife.

PROVERBS 5:15

My pillow was wet with tears after hearing that my boyfriend had cheated on me. It was my first real relationship in high school, and I had trusted this boy with my heart.

I vowed that I would never let that happen again. Instead of getting "played," I became a player, not caring about men's feelings. I tucked that woundedness deep down for no one to touch.

But God radically encountered me in my pain. He showed me that both men and women are created in His image, and to disrespect all men because of one boy wasn't honoring His intention.

The walls around my heart were blocking the opportunity for love, but God helped me learn to trust Him. He allowed me to meet Caleb and have my heart open and soft to him.

At times, past wounds have made me mistrust Caleb for reasons that had nothing to do with him. But God redeems even these things. We keep praying to have eyes only for each other, and God keeps healing us.

If you or your husband have ever struggled with trust, God wants to be part of the healing. He desires for you to have full purity in your marriage. He is worthy of our trust, and therefore we can have purity in the way we see our spouses.

Heavenly Father, You desire for my husband and me to have eyes only for You and each other. *Would You let my husband take full delight in me as his wife? Would You purify his eyes from any corruption of the world? Please help him have the wisdom and discernment to make wise choices in what he looks at, what he watches, and where he goes online. Please protect his eyes, mind, and heart from sexual sin. Keep cleansing his heart and mind, and let him see me through Your lens of love.*

Help me also to make wise decisions in what I choose to watch, listen to, and engage in. Let my thoughts be pure. Let my eyes delight only in my husband. I pray against any comparison, lust, or covetousness in our marriage.

Let us not lust after things of this world, but be filled by Your Word and truth. Help us to seek You first every single day. Amen.

Let my eyes be fixed on Jesus, and help my husband and me have eyes only for each other.

love in action . . .

Together: Plan a date night without any screens. Show each other attention and affection.

For him: Celebrate your husband's uniqueness. Articulate the specific ways God has made him special.

WITHERING AWAY

A prayer for rest

Jesus said, "Come to me, all of you who are weary and carry heavy burdens, and I will give you rest. Take my yoke upon you. Let me teach you, because I am humble and gentle at heart, and you will find rest for your souls."

MATTHEW 11:28-29

God put a call on my heart to share the gospel online and encourage people in their marriages. But neither Caleb nor I knew a thing about social media or business. Caleb was still teaching full-time and helping me on nights and weekends. We took classes on business, social media, and photography, and we were working hard to ensure our success and to eventually be able to work full-time together.

We knew that the more we engaged on social media, the more traction and followers we would get, and we weren't great at setting limits for ourselves. We were both so tired, and the time spent online was taking a toll on our relationship with God and each other.

About that time, we went to a marriage retreat where they invited us to put our phones away for four days. That felt like a lifetime, but we decided to trust God. What good would we be at helping others if we were withering from overwork?

God spoke clearly that we needed to take weekends off from social media for good. Our business may not have grown quite as fast, but Caleb was soon able to start working full-time with me. Each time we are obedient to God's call to rest in Him, we see the fruits in our souls and our relationship.

Dear heavenly Father, thank You for my husband. *There are times I see him so worn out and burdened. I pray for a deep soul rest for him. Help him make it a priority to rest physically, mentally, and emotionally. Help me create a safe space at home so he can get deep soul rest with You without me asking him for anything. If my husband has a hard time resting, help me not to nag or frustrate him further, but let the example of my own actions inspire him.*

Help us create rhythms in our marriage—time each day to rest in Your presence. May we set all our burdens into Your loving hands each night. Help us set aside one day a week for full rest from the work of our hands. May we trust You to provide and know that when we rest in You, You give us the wisdom, strength, and endurance to do what You've called us to in the coming week. You're the God who renews our strength and makes us run and not grow weary, walk and not be faint, as we put all our hope in You. Amen.

A soul at rest is one who has entrusted all burdens to God's faithful hands.

love in action . . .

Together: Before bed, breathe deeply. With each breath in, imagine God's love filling your soul. With every breath out, picture your burdens being placed in Jesus' hands.

For him: When you are tempted to pour out your worries to your husband, instead pour them out to God.

WEEK

6

CAN YOU HEAR ME?

A prayer for loving communication

Always be humble and gentle. Be patient with each other, making allowance for each other's faults because of your love. Make every effort to keep yourselves united in the Spirit, binding yourselves together with peace.

EPHESIANS 4:2-3

"I never heard you say that!" These words had become a familiar refrain in our marriage, an echo of past pain and insecurities.

For me, it stemmed from a lie I'd carried for so long that *My voice doesn't matter*. Caleb has always cared deeply about my thoughts and feelings. Yet that nagging lie persisted.

Complicating matters, Caleb has a hearing issue in his right ear. When I speak from behind him or when his head is turned, he may not hear me. One day, I asked Caleb to handle something important. I thought he had heard me, but it slipped through the cracks. Frustration welled up in me, and I confronted him.

"I never heard you say that!" His response hung in the air, thick with tension.

Instead of letting anger consume us, we chose patience and understanding. It was about more than just hearing words; it was about understanding each other's heart. We decided to tell each other important things only while in the same room, and preferably while making eye contact. With these guidelines, our communication breakdowns have lessened.

We still have our moments of frustration, but we are practicing patience, forgiveness, and openhearted listening, ensuring that every word truly matters. When you experience a breakdown in communication, remember that every day you can grow to hear and understand your husband better.

Heavenly Father, I thank You for my husband. *Even though we don't always understand each other, would You help us be patient in our communication? Help us to be humble and gentle. Let us seek to understand each other more than to be right. Help us to be slow to speak, quick to listen, and slow to become angry.*

Even though sometimes we might as well be speaking different languages, I care about my husband and what he wants. Would You allow me to slow down and make sure I truly understand him? It hurts my heart when I feel like we are on different pages. Help us to be in unity, to speak clearly and kindly. When we misunderstand each other, give us both the patience to listen and articulate our thoughts in a way that could be helpful and not hurtful.

I'm sorry for the times our communication has had breakdowns. Thank You that each day is a chance for a fresh start. Give me ears to hear my husband, and give him ears to hear me. Most of all, let us both have ears to hear You. Amen.

Listening well is an act of love.

love in action . . .

Together: When discussing important matters, commit to being face-to-face and maintaining eye contact for clear communication.

For him: Make a deliberate effort to actively listen to your husband each time he talks to you.

WEEK

7

FILLING THE EMPTY PLACES

A prayer that he finds his worth in Christ

You are a chosen people. You are royal priests, a holy nation, God's very own possession. As a result, you can show others the goodness of God, for he called you out of the darkness into his wonderful light.

1 PETER 2:9

My tendency before meeting Jesus was to seek my worth from men. After meeting Christ, I became intentional about having those empty places filled only by Him.

But after Caleb and I got married, I found myself running to him for comfort before seeking encouragement from God. Caleb is an incredible husband, but he makes a terrible god.

I can see Caleb right in front of me, so it's easy to turn to him in times of doubt. But that puts way too much pressure on my marriage. When I go to God first, when I open His Word and listen to His truth, I'm filled with the knowledge that my value is unshakable in Christ. Then my husband's love is the icing on the cake, and I don't put the pressure of perfection on him. Making that switch helped me enjoy my marriage and my life more. I want those empty places filled by our amazing Father in heaven.

If you have moments this week when you need a reminder of your value, I encourage you to go to God first. Let His love rush over you. Let His truth sink deep into your heart. Then, when you talk with your husband from a place of overflowing love, his good words are a bonus.

Dear God, there are places in our hearts that only You can fill. *Please fill those empty spaces with Your amazing love today. The world tells my husband that he should get his worth from outside sources—his reputation, his work, the money in his bank account. But You call us to find our worth in You alone. Help my husband seek Your praise and not the praise of others. Would You fill up the empty places in His heart with Your love? Would You let him know that he is Your masterpiece, Your beloved child?*

When either of us is feeling rejected, let us hold close to the truth that You call us chosen. When others make us feel less than valuable, help us to know we are Your royal priesthood. I pray that our identity would be in You alone. Let us listen to You, walk with You, and talk with You. Help us to not conform to the patterns of this world but to look to You. Let us speak the worth of Christ into each other's hearts today. Thank You! Amen.

The Lord alone can fill the empty places in our hearts.

love in action . . .

Together: Attend a worship service or worship at home. Lift your hearts in praise that your worth is found in God alone.

For him: Pray for your husband's identity in Christ. Speak 1 Peter 2:9 out loud, replacing "you" with your husband's name.

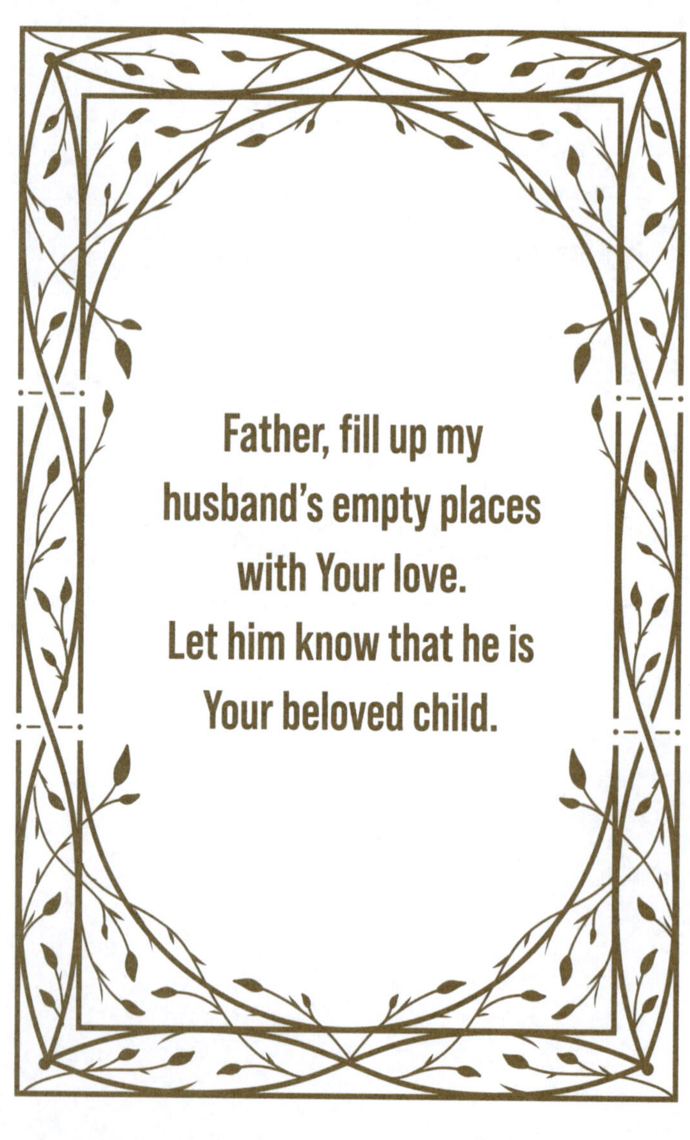
Father, fill up my
husband's empty places
with Your love.
Let him know that he is
Your beloved child.

LOST IN THE SAND

A prayer for forgiveness

Instead, be kind to each other, tenderhearted, forgiving one another, just as God through Christ has forgiven you.
EPHESIANS 4:32

For our honeymoon, Caleb and I traveled up and down California's beautiful Pacific Coast Highway. At one of our last stops, we had a romantic picnic on the beach.

Suddenly, Caleb noticed his wedding ring was missing. Our picnic turned to panic as we urgently hunted through the sand. A man with a metal detector joined the search, and he and Caleb spent some time looking around as I went back to our hotel room to wait. The sun was going down, and the beach had become quite cold. Wrapped in a blanket, I stood on the balcony and watched.

I had a choice: Would I blame and hold a grudge? Or would I let it go? I knew Caleb had not lost the ring on purpose and that we would look back and laugh about it someday. Thankfully, I chose the lighthearted, no-grudge option.

After I bought him another ring . . . and he lost it on a hike a few weeks later . . . I made the same choice: it's not a big deal. I ordered a pack of cheap silicone rings, which were perfect for my active husband.

I wish I could tell you this is how I handle every disappointment. But too often I've turned what could have been grace-filled moments into catastrophe. At those times, I can see Caleb sink into his shell. When I give him grace, he has wings to fly.

The many rings on his finger have all represented the same thing: the bond that can't be broken when God is at the center and we choose to let go of grievances. Holding Caleb's hand in mine today, I'm reminded that I want to let go of offenses, see the best in him, and extend grace.

Dear God, thank You that You paid our sin debt on the cross. *When we accept You, we no longer get what we deserve but are fully forgiven. Help us to live in gratitude every day, out of a deep rejoicing in our spirits because of Your goodness.*

I thank You for caring about me and my husband so much. Jesus, thank You that by Your wounds we are healed. I ask that You would keep healing any pain from the past or present in each of our lives. Help us to have compassion and forgiveness for each other. We know we can't do that without Your help. Please let grace abound where we need it. Thank You that You're the Great Physician and Mighty Counselor. Amen.

Forgiveness heals wounds and fortifies love; let go of grudges and choose to forgive.

love in action . . .

Together: Develop a forgiveness ritual to use when conflicts arise, whether holding hands, saying a forgiveness prayer, or simply hugging.

For him: Memorize Scripture verses on forgiveness, then speak them to yourself when tempted to hold a grudge.

WEEK

9

SEEKING GOD FIRST

A prayer for spiritual growth

Study this Book of Instruction continually. Meditate on it day and night so you will be sure to obey everything written in it. Only then will you prosper and succeed in all you do.

JOSHUA 1:8

Our first year of marriage was a big adjustment for me. I had fully given my life to Christ seven years prior, and I was hungry for God's Word first thing every day.

But when Caleb and I got married, I was shocked to see he didn't open his Bible in the morning. My husband was raised in the church and had a deep love for God. His actions reflected God's love to me and others. How was he not hungry for more?

I would nag him about seeking God first, communicating that he was letting me down. I saw a deeper hunger for football, video games, and TV shows than I did for God.

As time went on, I tried to nag less and pray more fervently. I saw Caleb going through the motions in life and knew he was meant for so much more.

Then God moved. Caleb had a radical encounter with Jesus and started getting real about past pain he had experienced in life and in the church. God began to heal those deep places. As Caleb became more passionate about his faith, more than about anything else, God placed a new calling and purpose on his life.

Dear God, thank You that You are the perfect example for my husband to look up to. *You are love. Everything good comes from You. I thank You that as my husband and I mature in Christ, we become more like You. I pray that You would give my husband a hunger for Your Word. May he meditate on Your truth and obey it. I want him to thrive, and as he trusts in Your Word, I know he will. Help him to crave Your Word and Your presence. Let him cry out to You when he is in need. Let Him seek You before anything else.*

Lord, I want to be an encouragement to my husband in this way. Would You help me not to nag him or pressure him but instead to be an example of what seeking You first looks like? If there's anything blocking my husband from wanting to grow closer to You, I pray that You would heal it. Amen.

Encourage each other's spiritual appetite and, together, thrive.

love in action . . .

Together: Begin keeping a journal of your prayers and the dates they are answered.

For him: Instead of nagging your husband about spiritual growth, commit to praying for him.

WEEK

10

SEEKING COMMUNITY

A prayer for healthy friendships

Let us think of ways to motivate one another to acts of love and good works. And let us not neglect our meeting together, as some people do, but encourage one another, especially now that the day of his return is drawing near.

HEBREWS 10:24-25

Friendships leave marks on our hearts—both of joy and of pain. They can leave us scarred and cautious. Caleb and I understand what it means to trust and then be betrayed. But God keeps healing and giving us new friends we cherish as we seek His wisdom.

There have been moments when it seemed easier to give up on friendship altogether, but I have such a deep desire for community. As Caleb and I venture into new friendships, we rely on each other's discernment and intuition. We've learned to recognize true friends from those who are self-serving.

Sometimes it's us making the first move in friendship—planning the parties, sending the invites, calling with a word of encouragement. But being intentional about friendship results in the gift of being known by others. It's not always easy, and sometimes our efforts seem unreciprocated, but we persist.

Through it all, Caleb and I remain steadfast friends to each other, nurturing our bond and sharing our hearts. True friendship is worth preserving and cherishing. My friendships with Jesus and with Caleb are my most precious treasures.

If you or your husband are bearing the scars of past friendships, do not lose hope. God is in the business of mending hearts, and He intends for us to do life walking alongside others.

Dear God, I pray that You would put people in my husband's life who are good for him and for our marriage. *Remove anyone who would hurt our marriage or my husband's life purpose. Please put men in his life who encourage him, speak the truth, and sharpen him to grow close to You, as he does the same for them. Help him to take the initiative in cultivating healthy friendships.*

Help us to be good friends to others, rejoicing with those who rejoice and weeping with those who weep. Let us never get jealous or compare. Help us to be there for a friend who is struggling, loving them like You do. Help us to see any rejection in friendship as Your protection and redirection. May we grow and learn from each experience and make friends who reflect Your love.

Lord, would You also grow the friendship between me and my husband? Let us be playful and fun together. Help us to delight in each other's interests and company. You are a friend that sticks closer than a brother. Help us to always find friendship with You. Amen.

Nurture your husband's friendships, knowing that good company builds character.

love in action . . .

Together: Plan a double-date night with another couple who share your faith and values.

For him: Surprise your husband with a thoughtful outing or activity that aligns with his interests.

WEEK

11

ONE-THOUSAND-FOOT DROP

A prayer for overcoming fears

Don't be afraid, for I am with you. Don't be discouraged, for I am your God. I will strengthen you and help you. I will hold you up with my victorious right hand.

ISAIAH 41:10

Caleb and I share a fear of heights. One summer, we faced and overcame that fear during a challenging yet awe-inspiring hike at Zion National Park in Utah.

The Angels Landing hike, known for its stunning views, had always intrigued us. But the thought of navigating a narrow path with a one-thousand-foot drop on either side, secured only by a cable, was daunting. We had contemplated this adventure for years but never quite found the courage until that summer.

Before the hike, I was filled with anxiety. But Caleb and I had made a pact: we would go at our own pace, support each other through every anxious moment, and turn back if either of us wanted to. We caught the bus to the trailhead and began our ascent, Caleb's reassuring presence giving me strength. Something about knowing we had to be brave for each other, and trusting that God was with us, made all the difference.

As we reached the cable section, an unexpected peace settled over us, and reaching the top was an exhilarating experience. The views were like a slice of heaven.

In marriage, we will often face challenges that seem insurmountable, with risks and dangers that can paralyze us. But with our husbands at our side, and with the knowledge of God's presence, navigating our fears becomes more manageable. That mutual reliance and trust make the journey a lot easier.

Dear heavenly Father, I lift up my husband to You, asking that You soothe any anxieties and replace his fears with Your peace. *At times, life's challenges can overwhelm him, stirring up worries about our future. In those moments, Lord, gently remind him of the countless blessings that surround him. Grant him the ability to see Your goodness in every situation, turning fear into a steadfast trust in You.*

Father, empower me to be a pillar of support for him—through prayer, service, encouragement, and simply being there. As he navigates trials, let him feel Your presence and my unwavering support, knowing he is not alone. I pray that he will not rely solely on his own strength. May he lean on You, trusting in Your ability to uplift and sustain him.

Your Word tells us that perfect love casts out fear. I pray that Your perfect love would envelop us, extinguishing any sparks of fear, and that we will find comfort and strength in Your truth. You are our loving Father, and I am endlessly thankful for the gift of my husband. Please grant him peace today and in the days to come. Amen.

When we face overwhelming fear, God's love is a secure foundation.

love in action . . .

Together: When fear seems overwhelming, make a plan for facing it head-on.

For him: If your husband is facing fears, let him know you care about his concerns and are there to support him.

FANNING THE SPARKS

A prayer for intimacy and romance

Let him kiss me with the kisses of his mouth—
for your love is more delightful than wine.
SONG OF SONGS 1:2, NIV

Several years ago, in our California apartment, Caleb told me to wait upstairs. I could tell he was doing something special. But when I heard a loud noise, I peeked over the banister to see six-foot flames on our porch!

I sprinted down the stairs and out the front door to find one of the apartment complex fire extinguishers, crashed open the box, and put out the fire with Caleb. It turned out that sweet Caleb had lit the tiki torches, and an ember had fallen on the outdoor furniture cushions.

He had planned a beautiful porch date for us, but the spark he was trying to light got a little too hot. Since no one was hurt, we laughed and laughed. We still had the most romantic evening, and I felt so cherished.

I've found that the more we cherish each other, the more our love grows. The spark doesn't look the same as on our honeymoon, but I like our romance even better now. As we embrace our differences, learn each other's likes and dislikes, and strive to be intentional in our actions, I truly believe love can grow.

Even if you feel like the spark is gone in your marriage, I encourage you to begin treating your husband like an amazing treasure from God. See only his good qualities and build him up in love. The smallest efforts—even if they don't go as planned!—will make him feel like a hero.

Dear God, help me to understand the things that make my husband feel loved and desired. *When we don't seem to be in sync, help us learn to love the other the way they desire. Let us rejoice in our differences and never let them divide us. Help us to never shame one another, but always encourage.*

I know that intimacy is created in big and small moments throughout the day. Help me to see ordinary moments as opportunities to show my husband love in a way that speaks to him. Let him be intoxicated with my love, and me with his love. Let us delight in each other's bodies and company, and let us have eyes only for each other. May we be careful about where we go, what we look at, what we watch. If anything is causing us to look another way, let us say no and be drawn back together.

Help us to pursue and adore each other. Help us to find moments for romance. As we grow older, let every day tie our souls closer together. Let our love continually grow as we are intentional about keeping romance alive. Amen.

Cherish the unique qualities that make your husband extraordinary. Nurture the intimacy that blossoms every day.

love in action . . .

Together: Create opportunities for intimacy throughout the day with passionate kisses, tender touches, and affectionate words.

For him: Express your admiration for your husband's exceptional attributes and let him know how deeply you value his distinctiveness.

WEEK

13

BETTER THAN GPS

A prayer for wise decisions

Fear of the LORD is the foundation of wisdom.
Knowledge of the Holy One results in good judgment.
PROVERBS 9:10

Caleb and I were presented with an amazing opportunity for our business. It was the biggest breakthrough we'd had up to that point. But for some reason, we lacked peace about saying yes.

We made a list, and the pros far outweighed the cons. I asked my Bible study to pray about the opportunity, and they thought it was an incredible blessing. But we still couldn't shake the lack of peace. I kept feeling like God was telling me to say no, and when I told this to Caleb, he said, "Even if all the wise counsel is saying yes, if God says no, it needs to be a no."

So we turned down the opportunity. My friends thought we were crazy. That is, until something *really* crazy happened.

Just a month later, the whole world shut down, and that amazing opportunity never came to be because of the pandemic. If we had said yes, we would have put in time and energy, only to be let down.

There's no way we could have foreseen the events of 2020, but God knew. His wisdom is greater than any human understanding. This experience strengthened our faith and determination to listen to God and seek His wisdom above all else.

Dear God, the fear of You is the beginning of wisdom. *Let us keep seeking You and knowing You more. We know this results in good judgment. My husband makes so many decisions every day, and all of them affect me and our marriage. Would You give him guidance in even the smallest decisions? Let him long to hear Your voice and be obedient when You say, "This is the way; walk in it." Would You let him hold Your hand like a dependent child walking step-by-step with his heavenly Father?*

Lord, any time my husband makes a decision I don't agree with, help me trust You. Let me speak the truth in love, but not complain. Help me to go to You in prayer, knowing You can rework even our mistakes for our good. You are better than GPS, so each time we make a wrong turn, You can reroute us quickly. Help both of us seek Your wisdom. Let Your words guide our steps. Thank You that when we ask You, You show us the way to go. Amen.

God is better than GPS. Listen to His voice and let Him guide your steps.

love in action . . .

Together: Dedicate time to reading God's Word together. Allow its wisdom to guide your decisions.

For him: Show grace and patience when your husband faces decisions, knowing that learning to recognize God's wisdom is a lifelong journey.

Father, help us
to pursue and adore
each other. Help us
to find moments
for romance. Let each
day tie our souls
closer together.

WEEK

14

AN UNEXPECTED SITUATION

A prayer for love and respect

Love each other with genuine affection, and take delight in honoring each other.

ROMANS 12:10

"No one is going to like you if you keep talking that highly about your husband." My friend's words left me stunned. She shared that some women were talking about me and how they disliked my habit of speaking so positively about Caleb.

But I refused to compromise my respect and honor for my husband just to gain friends. My response was clear: "I will never speak ill of Caleb."

This choice came at a cost, as I lost some friends along the way. But as my friend continued to share dishonoring stories about her husband, her friendships grew. This led to another hard decision: not to keep people in my life who speak negatively about their spouses.

If you choose to honor and respect your husband, you may find yourself going against the grain. While others complain about their spouses, your decision to hold your tongue could make you feel like an outcast.

But honoring your husband is a powerful choice. It strengthens your marriage, deepens your connection with your husband, and sets a standard of love and respect that others may come to admire and follow. In a world that encourages negativity, your commitment to honor and respect will be a beacon of light and an example of the qualities that God desires in marriage.

Dear heavenly Father, You are worthy of all our honor and respect. *Thank You that You made my husband in Your image and likeness. I pray that he would walk in a way that would be worthy of respect from all he encounters. Mature him each day to be more like You. Help him be respectful of others, and let him be a man of honor and integrity who lives above reproach. I pray that when he falls short, he can receive Your forgiveness and not hold on to shame. Let him walk in the newness of life that You offer.*

Give me eyes to see the best in my husband, and help me call forth the best in him. When I disagree with him or feel frustrated, would You help me to extend grace and kindness? Please give me the words to say or the wisdom to hold my tongue.

Help my husband also to have a deep, growing respect for me. Help him to speak and think kindly of me, both when I am present and when I am not, and may I do the same. Help us to outdo each other in honor. Let our love and respect be genuine as we seek to honor You. Amen.

In a world where negativity prevails, let your respect for your husband shine as a powerful example.

love in action . . .

Together: Commit to always speaking positively about each other in public and in private.

For him: The next time you are in a public setting, honor your husband by sharing something wonderful about him.

WEEK

15

CRUSHED DREAMS

A prayer for enduring faith

We can rejoice, too, when we run into problems and trials, for we know that they help us develop endurance. And endurance develops strength of character, and character strengthens our confident hope of salvation.

ROMANS 5:3-4

Caleb lay on the couch in so much pain. He had irritated a back injury from his college basketball days, but the pain was more than physical. I knew he was reliving the wounds of his crushed dreams.

Caleb had dreamed of playing basketball his whole life. He would practice for hours with his team, then shoot a thousand more baskets. He got a basketball scholarship and kept working hard. Hearing his stories, I could see his endurance and determination. He gave up so much to make his dream a reality. Until that career-ending injury.

"God is still good," Caleb said. "I didn't claim that truth back in college, but I choose it now. He's good in my best moments and my worst."

I saw Caleb's back grow stronger each day, but I also saw him endure in trusting God through the pain. He chose to worship God through the trial, and he reached a deeper layer of healing by being honest with God about his feelings.

As wives, we hate seeing our husbands suffer. But we need to trust that God can use *all* things for good. Let's keep praying that through the trials they would endure in faith and grow in love for God.

Dear heavenly Father, it breaks my heart to think of the trials my husband has had to endure. *I thank You for his resilience. Would You stick close to him and give him perseverance to endure hard things? Would You give him a deep knowledge of Your truth so that through the trials he grows stronger and more like You? Lord, let those difficult experiences strengthen his character and his hope that You will one day redeem the world.*

Help me to be a source of encouragement for him to keep pursuing You through the good and bad. Speak through me, and let Your presence fill our marriage. Help us to stick by each other's side through all life brings. Keep us from getting discouraged or losing hope. Remind us that when we patiently endure trials and testing, we will receive a crown from You. Thank You that You never leave us. You have been with us through the best moments, and You carry us through the hardest trials. We need You, Lord. Help our relationship with You and each other to endure and grow stronger daily. Amen.

Through every trial we will cling to Jesus, our source of strength, and together, we'll endure and grow stronger.

love in action . . .

Together: Attend a charity event or volunteer together, reminding each other of the importance of enduring challenges for a greater purpose.

For him: Surprise your husband with a small care package of encouraging notes, favorite snacks, and a verse about endurance.

WEEK

16

SILVER LININGS

A prayer for assuming the best in each other

Test everything that is said. Hold on to what is good. Stay away from every kind of evil.

1 THESSALONIANS 5:21-22

As a newlywed, I was taken aback by Caleb's unwavering positivity. He could find the silver lining in every situation. I considered myself an optimist, but Caleb was on a whole different level.

At first, I didn't quite know how to handle it. Was he being naive or overly optimistic? Eventually, I realized the incredible blessing Caleb's positivity is. His ability to assume the best in people, including me, is a breath of fresh air. He radiates grace and understanding, even in the face of challenges.

Early on, though, his positivity sometimes made me feel like my concerns were being overlooked. I would take offense or jump to conclusions, yet he would forgive me so quickly. Caleb learned to spend time listening and to show he understands my struggles instead of immediately pointing out the silver lining. This has helped me feel heard, known, and loved.

Even so, I want to follow his example in focusing on the good. At one pivotal moment, I sensed God telling me not to say or think anything negative about Caleb. As I began to focus on his strengths and the countless ways he showed his love, I felt a profound healing within our marriage.

This doesn't mean we have to avoid addressing real issues. It means we assume the best more often and speak the truth in love so we can fight the *problem* instead of fighting each other.

Dear God, thank You for the tremendous blessing of getting to do this life next to my husband. *I know one of the evil one's greatest tricks is to get us to view each other as the enemy. I pray that this wouldn't be so for us. Would You help us to assume the best about the other's words, thoughts, and actions? I pray that no root of offense or bitterness would establish itself in our hearts. Please help my husband to resist any negative thought about me or our marriage. Help him to draw close to You and have his eyes fixed on You.*

Please also empower me to fix my thoughts on what is true, holy, excellent, and praiseworthy. I'm sorry for the times I have jumped to conclusions or taken offense at my husband's tone of voice or action. Thank You for Your forgiveness, Lord. Would You help me to move forward in seeing my husband through Your lens of love? Let me dwell on things that are worthy of praise and let go of anything negative. Amen.

Choose to see the best in each other, for you are both precious gifts from God.

love in action . . .

Together: Look into each other's eyes and list three things you love about the other person. Let the words sink in.

For him: When your mind moves toward the negative about your husband, replace it with something praiseworthy. Let your actions overflow from that outlook.

WEEK
17

CHECKUP TIME

A prayer for clarity and direction

The Lord says, "I will guide you along the best pathway for your life. I will advise you and watch over you."
PSALM 32:8

Caleb and I share a little green journal, a treasure that has journeyed with us through the years of our marriage. We started this tradition our very first year together, with eager hearts and high hopes.

Every year, we sit in a cozy coffee shop, the green journal between us. Inside are dedicated pages for each area of life: Faith, Friendships, Family, Finances, Fitness, and, of course, our Relationship.

We scribble down the things we cherished in the past year, the moments that made our hearts sing, and the challenges we faced. But more than just recounting the past, it is about seeking God's wisdom for the future. Holding hands and with our foreheads touching, we pray for guidance in every aspect of our lives. We check in with God about where we are on the right track and where we need to walk more in step with Him.

Then, in the green journal, we set tangible, attainable goals that will lead us closer to the dreams we whispered to God. And you know what's incredible? Over the years, so many of those dreams have come to fruition.

Our green journal is our surrender to God's will and direction. He's redirected us often, but He keeps us in unity as He continues working on both of our hearts.

Heavenly Father, I lift up to You my husband's goals and direction and the need for clarity in his life. *Inspire him to continue growing, especially in the pursuit of his dreams. Please reveal any areas where he may have resisted growth or where he feels uncertain. Break any strongholds that may be keeping him from moving forward in confidence.*

Father, I ask that You develop a strong sense of purpose and clarity in my husband's heart and mind. Help him discern Your will and the path You have set before him. Guide him in making decisions that align with Your divine plan for him.

Show me how I can support him in this journey—whether through words of encouragement, actions, or even practical support. May our partnership be a source of strength and unity as we both seek to grow and fulfill our purpose.

Lord, I also pray that You would help me never to be complacent with my own life and goals. May our love and commitment to each other continue to deepen as we pursue our individual and shared goals. Thank You for blessing me with such a wonderful partner and best friend. Amen.

You can grow in ways you never thought possible when you set goals together, with God's guidance.

love in action . . .

Together: As a couple, keep a journal for checking in with God in every area of your life.

For him: Give your husband a journal for capturing his thoughts, dreams, and reflections on seeking God's wisdom in life decisions.

WEEK

18

PERFECT TIMING

A prayer for persistence in seeking God

Keep on asking, and you will receive what you ask for. Keep on seeking and you will find. Keep on knocking, and the door will be opened to you.

MATTHEW 7:7

In a challenging financial season, Caleb and I found ourselves in a tight spot. Unexpected bills seemed to multiply, and most of our income depended on project-based work, leaving us anxiously waiting for payments.

During this time, we received a message from someone I had met on a missions trip to Rwanda. A woman who had helped out for years at the orphanage there needed financial support so her daughter could attend school. We sensed God's call to step out in faith and help, and we prayed fervently, trusting that God would provide for us as well.

As our finances remained precarious, it felt like walking a tightrope of faith. We wondered if God was going to come through. Slowly but surely, He began to show up in unexpected ways. Clients paid their invoices, work opportunities emerged, and we received unexpected financial blessings.

God used that season to refine our character, deepen our persistence, and strengthen our faith. His faithfulness knows no bounds, and His provision is not limited by our circumstances.

Dear friend, if you are fervently praying and waiting for God's provision—whether financially, spiritually, or relationally—don't lose heart. His timing is always perfect. Keep trusting, keep persisting in prayer. God is working in ways you may not fully understand, but His faithfulness remains unwavering.

Dear God, thank You that You are a God who sees and hears us. *Thank You for answering so many of our prayers. I ask that my husband would be persistent in prayer and action. Help him not to give up. Let him keep asking, seeking, and knocking, and help me to do the same. Like the persistent widow who kept asking until she got what she needed, we know that You want to fill our lives with good things. Help us to count our blessings and see the ways You are working.*

Father, help us to be patient when we face troubles, trusting in Your perfect timing. We offer You all our troubles right now, handing each one over to Your faithful hands. You've called us to be persistent in trusting You and Your goodness. Please keep strengthening both of us in this area. Amen.

Be persistent in prayer. At the right time, God will move.

love in action . . .

Together: Create a prayer corner where you can post the things that need persistent prayer.

For him: Write a love letter highlighting your husband's strengths and expressing your admiration for his persistence.

WEEK

19

LAYING DOWN OUR PRIDE

A prayer for humility

Don't be selfish; don't try to impress others. Be humble, thinking of others as better than yourselves. Don't look out only for your own interests, but take an interest in others, too.

PHILIPPIANS 2:3-4

When we were first married, there were so many times I was convinced I was right. I would go to great lengths to prove it—even if it meant belittling my husband or making him feel inadequate. I hate to type that, but it's true. It was my way of trying to prove my own worth.

Pride may be the biggest killer of marriages and happiness. It blinds us to our own faults and makes us unwilling to consider another person's perspective. But there are always two sides to a story, and each person's experience is valid.

God has been teaching me to lay down my pride, to be comfortable saying, "Let's agree to disagree," and to truly listen without pushing my own agenda. I'm not perfect at this, especially in the heat of the moment, but God is faithful in His pruning process.

The beautiful thing about humility is that it mirrors the character of Jesus Himself. He laid down His life for us, considering our needs above His own. He didn't need to prove His greatness; He simply loved and served.

Embracing humility is not about keeping score or proving a point; it's about loving and lifting one another up. Let's learn from Jesus' example and let humility be the cornerstone of our relationships.

Dear faithful Father, thank You that You are the perfect example for me and my husband. *Help my husband to do nothing out of selfish ambition or vanity, but to consider others' needs before his own. Help him to look not just to his own interests, but also the interests of others. Even at times when I am sensitive, let his tone be kind and his touch be soft, and let me feel his gentle humility toward me. Help pride to be pruned from his life and relationships.*

God, I pray that I would be a wife who seeks to understand more than to prove I'm right. I'm so sorry for the ways I've fought to be right instead of laying down my pride. I pray that I would be less selfish and more like You. Let me look at my husband's interests even above my own. You will provide all my needs and hear all my concerns. I can trust that as I grow in humility, You will exalt me at the right time. Let humility keep growing in our relationship. Thank You, God! Amen.

Choose humility in your marriage, and watch it flourish. Pride hinders, but humility brings wisdom and blessing.

love in action . . .

Together: Commit to being quick to apologize without excuses or defensiveness.

For him: When disagreements arise, practice saying, "Let's agree to disagree" instead of pushing your point.

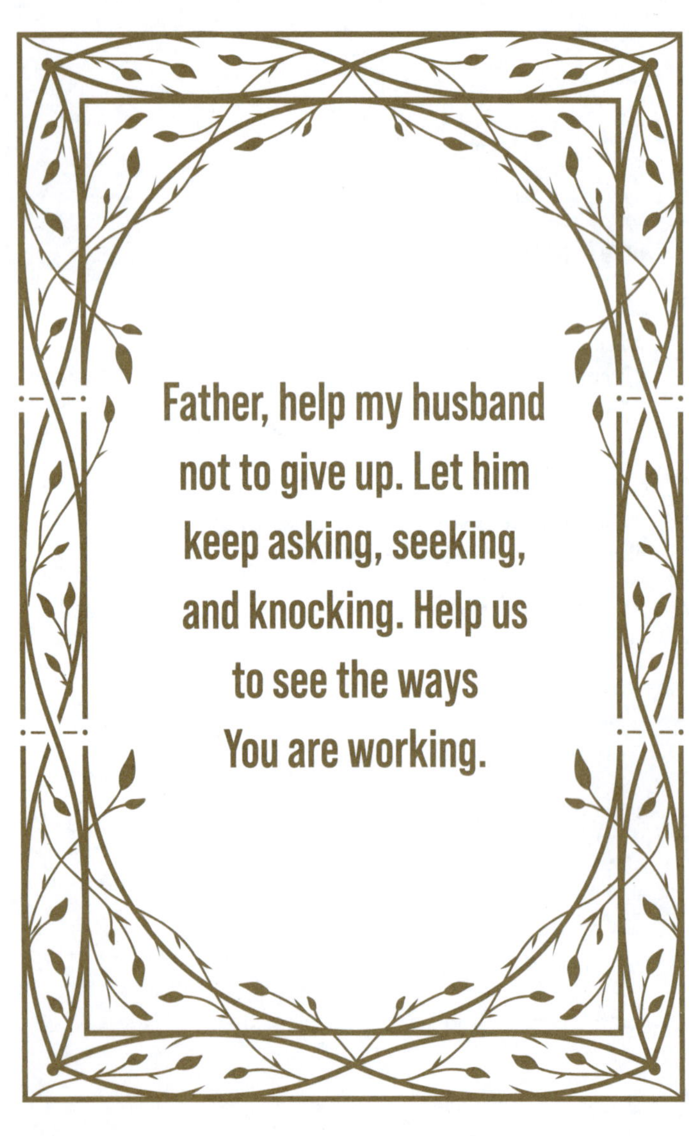

Father, help my husband not to give up. Let him keep asking, seeking, and knocking. Help us to see the ways You are working.

WEEK

20

PAINFUL REVELATION

A prayer for growing trust in God and each other

When I am afraid, I will put my trust in you. I praise God for what he has promised. I trust in God, so why should I be afraid?

PSALM 56:3-4

During a challenging period in our relationship, Caleb and I embarked on a marriage retreat at Hume Lake in California. We felt disconnected, but the reasons remained elusive. When the retreat leaders encouraged us to take a walk and share any secrets we had been keeping, the truth began to unfold.

Caleb bravely confessed that he had been withholding things from me. He felt I was too controlling, and he feared my reaction. It was a painful revelation, but a necessary one. As we walked, the weight of my controlling tendencies pressed down on me. I had held on so tight because I thought that was the way to be safe and not get hurt. But it was having the opposite effect.

Then came a trust exercise on the ropes course, where we had to jump off a high platform. Fear gripped me, and tears flowed. I didn't trust the pulley system. But God wanted me to release the control that was suffocating my marriage and my relationship with Him. I made the jump, and I trembled in Caleb's arms with tears of surrender. I apologized for stifling our marriage and hindering honest conversations. Our marriage began to flourish as trust in God and each other deepened.

Dear sister, take courage. Trust God to guide you both toward vulnerability, openness, and trust. He can rebuild trust, and He is faithful to catch us every time.

Dear heavenly Father, please help my husband to be a man of integrity who is worthy of trust and honor. *Let him be someone his friends can depend on, and help him to be a trustworthy husband with his words and actions. Let him follow through on his promises. If my husband has any mistrust of You because of pain from the past, would You heal those wounds so he would put his trust in You again? In any area where he has broken Your trust or mine, would You convict him and restore him once again?*

Lord, I desire to be a wife that my husband can trust. In any way I have broken Your trust or his, would You restore me? I don't wish to be a controlling wife. Help me to release my grip and place my hope in You. Help us not to rely on ourselves. Let us rely on You above all else, even when we are afraid. Please give my husband and me the courage to trust You completely, releasing the need for control. Help us walk in vulnerability and openness, relying on Your love and guidance to strengthen our bond. Amen.

As I release control into God's hands, my trust grows—in Him and in my husband.

love in action . . .

Together: Look into going on a marriage retreat to enrich your relationship.

For him: When you feel the need to control your husband, retrain your mind that it is safe to trust God with your heart.

WEEK

21

UNCOMFORTABLE SPACES

A prayer for emotional support

The purposes of a person's heart are deep waters,
but one who has insight draws them out.
PROVERBS 20:5, NIV

The heart of every person is a well of emotions, complex and intricate as the depths of the sea. It can be challenging to navigate these waters, especially in the context of marriage.

My husband, Caleb, is a wonderful man, logical and practical. Early in our marriage, when I was emotionally distraught, he'd often respond with facts and reasoning, thinking he could "fix" my feelings by showing me they didn't make sense. In reality, it often made my distress worse. I felt invalidated and guilty for feeling sad or upset.

But over time, something beautiful happened. Caleb began to grow in his ability to stay with me in the uncomfortable space of sadness. He learned to carry my pain with me, to hold me close, and to assure me that my feelings were valid. It was a transformation in our relationship, one that allowed me to be vulnerable and share my emotions more openly.

However, I've come to realize that while our husbands can be amazingly supportive, they are not a substitute for our Mighty Counselor, Jesus. He sits with us, listens to us, and offers us His boundless comfort and understanding. In those times when Caleb is unable to show up for me in the way I long for, it has drawn me closer to Jesus, my true source of emotional support.

Dear heavenly Father, thank You for creating us with complex emotions and for providing the support we need, both through each other and through Your unwavering presence. *I pray that my husband and I would continue to grow in our ability to be emotionally supportive of one another.*

Help us to be understanding and patient and to draw out each other's feelings rather than trying to fix them. Give us the grace to sit with one another in times of distress, to offer a listening ear, a comforting touch, and the assurance that our emotions are valid.

Lord, I also recognize that You are the ultimate source of comfort and understanding. In moments when our earthly support falls short, may we turn to You, our Mighty Counselor, who knows our hearts intimately and offers boundless love and compassion. Amen.

It's okay not to have all the answers. A listening ear and a comforting presence can make a world of difference.

love in action . . .

Together: Plan a peaceful nature walk together, allowing the serene surroundings to create a calm atmosphere for heartfelt conversation.

For him: Practice active listening by asking your husband open-ended questions and being genuinely attentive to the response.

WEEK

22

ON THE SAME TEAM

A prayer for resolving conflicts with grace

Don't repay evil for evil. Don't retaliate with insults when people insult you. Instead, pay them back with a blessing. That is what God has called you to do, and he will grant you his blessing.

1 PETER 3:9

As newlyweds, Caleb and I faced our share of conflict. Disagreements would escalate, and we would go to bed angry, carrying our grievances into the next day. The unresolved issues were taking a toll.

One evening, we retreated to our separate corners, simmering in anger. But a gentle conviction settled over us, and we each called out to God for help. He became the middle ground, and we began to see each other through His lens. We realized that harboring anger only invited discord into our home.

Talking about our feelings in a kind, compassionate, we-are-a-team way really changed things. We talked openly about our feelings, and we listened to each other's perspectives without defending ourselves.

I also learned not to go to Caleb in the heat of anger, which only triggered defensiveness in him. I began processing my feelings with God first, and then going to Caleb in a more peaceful state.

The atmosphere in our home shifted from hostility to grace as we learned to fight the problem and not each other. Conflict resolution is not easy, but it's essential for a healthy relationship. When we see our husbands as part of our team, assume the best about them, and are real and honest with God, we are more likely to find peace.

Dear heavenly Father, thank You for the wisdom and guidance in Your Word regarding conflict resolution. *Help us to go to You first when we feel overwhelmed so we can approach each other in a calmer manner that is easier for the other person to receive.*

We grew up learning to handle conflict in certain ways. Lord, if those ways do not honor You, please enable us to handle conflicts according to Your Word and not our past. When we fall back into old patterns, help us to give grace to each other.

Lord, we want no root of bitterness to take hold in our marriage. Would You give us eyes to see each other out of compassion and love? Would You help us to be humble and quick to forgive? Teach us to be quick to listen and slow to speak when conflicts arise. Let our words be filled with kindness and understanding, producing the righteousness that You desire. Help us to be peacemakers in our relationship and to extend blessing, even when we feel wronged.

I pray for Your continued guidance and grace as we navigate conflicts together. Help us to see each other as a team, always assuming the best. Amen.

You, your husband, and God are a team. Keep Him at the center as you seek to resolve conflict.

love in action . . .

Together: Commit to a time-out when things get elevated. Remember you are on the same team, assume the best, and allow God's love to overflow.

For him: Go to God first when you're overwhelmed with emotion. Then go to your husband in a peaceful, calm way.

WEEK

23

REALITY CHECK

A prayer for wise financial stewardship

Honor the Lord with your wealth and with the best part of everything you produce. Then he will fill your barns with grain, and your vats will overflow with good wine.

PROVERBS 3:9-10

Caleb and I were full of dreams in our first year of marriage. We had plans to buy a house, start a family, and live the American dream. However, reality hit hard when we realized our combined salaries were far from enough to achieve our goals.

We had to shift our perspective and ask God what truly mattered. With the help of a financial adviser, we learned to budget, set attainable goals, and break free from money-related strongholds. It's easy to make decisions based solely on finances, but that doesn't bring life. We needed to continually seek God's guidance and correction.

As we confronted our spending patterns, we discovered a poverty mindset, wrong attitudes about self-worth, and the allure of material possessions. But we also learned that we could use money as a tool to fulfill God's purposes, bless others, and build His Kingdom.

Miraculously, we are now sitting in our own home, a testimony to God's provision. Blessings can come in humbling ways, and it's an ongoing journey to trust God as our ultimate Provider.

Money can be a source of contention in marriages due to differing backgrounds and perspectives. But as we choose to pray and seek God's perspective, He will shape our hearts, guide our financial decisions, and unify our goals.

Dear heavenly Father, help my husband to be honest, trustworthy, wise, and generous with our finances. *Help him to surrender our financial worries and anxieties to You, trusting that You will provide for our needs according to Your riches in glory. May his desires align with Your will, so that we are storing up treasures in heaven, where nothing can destroy or steal them.*

Keep him from the love of money, which can lead to all kinds of evil. Instead of seeking wealth for its own sake, may he seek Your Kingdom and righteousness first. Help him to keep his eyes on You as our ultimate Provider. Teach him to steward our finances wisely and generously, using them to bless others and advance Your Kingdom. Break any strongholds and wrong mindsets he may have about money, and help him to view it through Your lens.

May we as a couple continually seek Your guidance in financial decisions and trust that You will provide for our needs. Keep our hearts humble and focused on what truly matters. May our financial decisions reflect our love for You and our desire to obey Your Word. In Jesus' name, I pray. Amen.

**Money is a tool for God's purposes.
Use it wisely to honor Him.**

love in action . . .

Together: Set a budget and attainable goals for your future. Seek financial advice, if needed.

For him: Reflect on anything you've been holding against your husband in the area of money. Choose to release and forgive today.

Father, help us
to remember that love
is a choice we make
over and over. Protect
my husband from
anything that would
draw his love away.

WEEK

24

KNOWING SMILES

A prayer for persevering love

Many waters cannot quench love, nor can rivers drown it.

SONG OF SONGS 8:7

Caleb and I had just tied the knot when I started working with him at the Christian school. Our classrooms were on opposite sides of the building, but we would bring each other a snack or leave a sweet note. Our colleagues gave us knowing smiles.

"Don't get used to it," they'd say. "It's just newlywed bliss."

But we were convinced our love was built on a foundation stronger than mere infatuation. Sure enough, the kindness hasn't stopped. We realized early on that love is more than a fleeting emotion; it's a conscious choice we make every day.

One thing that has helped is understanding each other's love languages. We actively practice acts of service, quality time, words of affirmation, physical touch, and giving and receiving gifts.[2] These intentional gestures have kept our love alive and thriving.

Love isn't just a feeling; it's a promise to cherish and care for each other, no matter what. Love is patient and kind, it doesn't keep a record of wrongs, and it endures through every circumstance. God's love holds us together.

---

[2] For more about the love languages, see Gary Chapman, *The 5 Love Languages*, especially chapters 4–8.

Dear heavenly Father, help me to remember that love is not just a fleeting emotion but a choice we make over and over. *Would You allow my husband to grow in love for me each day? Even as we age, let our love grow deeper. Help him to have eyes only for me, and protect him from anything that would draw his love away from me. May he be patient and kind, humble and gentle, and always willing to forgive. Let him not keep a record of wrongs, but instead, let love cover a multitude of sins.*

Give us the wisdom to cherish and nurture the love we have for each other. May we always find delight in honoring and serving one another. Any time our love tanks are low, help us to love the way we did at first—with so much intention, care, and consideration. Let us never take each other for granted.

In times of conflict or hardship, help us to endure, for love never gives up. Let our love be a testimony of Your enduring love for us. Amen.

Love is not just a feeling. It's a daily choice to cherish and care for each other.

love in action . . .

Together: Discover each other's love languages and intentionally express love in those ways.

For him: Be intentional about loving your husband the way you did when you first fell in love.

WEEK

25

STRIKING A BALANCE

A prayer for healthy boundaries with in-laws

"God made them male and female" from the beginning of creation. "This explains why a man leaves his father and mother and is joined to his wife, and the two are united into one." Since they are no longer two but one, let no one split apart what God has joined together.

MARK 10:6-9

For the first eight years of our marriage, Caleb and I lived in Southern California, close to his parents and brother. Their joyful, fun-loving dispositions were infectious, and in my eagerness to be a good daughter-in-law, I said yes to every invite.

But in doing so, I put a lot of pressure on myself. I didn't want to disappoint them. With all my new roles—new job, new wife, new living situation—I soon found myself burned out.

One pivotal conversation with my mother-in-law transformed our dynamic. We decided to use a scale from 1 to 10 to assess the importance of each event or invitation. If it ranked 1 to 5, it was a kind gesture, but there was no obligation to attend. For 6 to 10, we would make an effort to attend, depending on importance.

Our new approach allowed Caleb and me to invest quality time in our marriage while cherishing special family moments. Striking a balance between loving your spouse's family and setting boundaries is vital for a harmonious marriage and in-law relationship. Embrace the uniqueness of your spouse's family, and remember that love, kindness, and grace are your greatest allies.

Dear heavenly Father, I pray for my husband today. *Would You help him navigate how to be a good son-in-law and a good son? Help him in leaving his family and cleaving to me—still honoring them but setting the proper boundaries to put You first and me next. You wish to fill us with wonderful relationships, but there is also a great attack against relationships. Would You keep offenses from marinating in our in-law relationships? May we see the best in one another and make allowance for our faults.*

We thank You for the families we have married into, each with its own set of values and traditions. We seek Your wisdom and guidance to foster understanding and harmony. Help us to honor each other's families with love, kindness, and grace. Give us the discernment to recognize the unspoken rules and navigate the challenges that may arise. May we always prioritize our marriage as we navigate these intricate relationships. We lift up our in-laws with gratitude for the love they extend to us. May our interactions be filled with love and mutual respect, strengthening the bonds within our families. Amen.

Marriage is a dance of love, and in-law relationships are an integral part of the melody.

love in action . . .

Together: Consider using the 1 to 10 scale with your in-laws to evaluate the importance of family events and invitations.

For him: To strengthen your in-law relationships, tell your husband any unwritten rules about your family and ask if there are any for his.

WEEK

26

BREAK-IN

A prayer for protective boundaries

"I have the right to do anything," you say—but not everything is beneficial. "I have the right to do anything"—but not everything is constructive.

1 CORINTHIANS 10:23, NIV

Caleb and I lived in a charming condo in California. It was a God-sent gift, half the price of others in the area. However, there was one drawback. There was no protection for the cars parked below. No garage door, no gate, nothing.

Our trusty old Suburban, boasting over 200,000 miles, sat amid newer cars with alarm systems. An easy target, it was broken into at least five times. But one day I went to get in our car and found it entirely gone!

Just as our car was vulnerable, neglecting boundaries in marriage can leave our relationships susceptible to harm. Without diligent safeguarding, we invite chaos and discord. Boundaries serve as protective gates, allowing love to flourish.

One little example of how Caleb and I use boundaries to protect our purity is being careful not to watch shows above a TV-14 rating (or PG-13 for movies). One show we were watching regularly was only rated TV-14, but several characters were very contentious with each other. Caleb recognized that the more we watched it, the more contentious we were becoming with each other. He suggested we not watch the show anymore, and I happily agreed.

It's important to have the wisdom to say no to anything harming our relationship with God or each other. Instead fill the space with something that will fill you up!

Heavenly Father, I acknowledge that boundaries are not meant to isolate us but to safeguard the precious union You've blessed us with. *Would You protect my husband's eyes, mind, heart, attention, and time? Would You give him wisdom about when to say yes and when to say no and the courage to follow through? Help him to set boundaries to protect our marriage in the friendships he invests in, the media he consumes, the way he spends his time, and the things that get his attention. Help him to be fervent in honoring You first and in placing me above any other earthly relationship.*

Please give us the insight to recognize where boundaries are necessary and the courage to establish them. Help us to understand that boundaries are a sign of love and respect for our marriage. May we be vigilant in ensuring they remain strong and thriving. Give us the strength and wisdom to keep destructive influences at bay while allowing the beauty of love to grow.

I pray for Your guidance, knowing that with Your wisdom, our marriage will glorify You. Amen.

Boundaries are not barriers to love but gatekeepers of its sanctity.

love in action . . .

Together: Consider whether you need to establish or adjust boundaries for the well-being of your relationship.

For him: Reflect on anything that could be causing division or causing you to think less of your husband. Set boundaries to protect your love.

WEEK

27

SPIRITUAL WORKOUT

A prayer for discipline and self-control

Prepare your minds for action and exercise self-control. Put all your hope in the gracious salvation that will come to you when Jesus Christ is revealed to the world.

1 PETER 1:13

As Caleb and I began our new ministry, our phones were our bedside companions. The temptation to check for notifications, likes, and shares was hard to resist first thing in the morning. Based on these worldly metrics, I found myself doubting the success of our work.

But Caleb reminded me that success is ultimately measured by God, not by the numbers on social media. He proposed a solution that required significant self-control: keeping our phones out of the bedroom and dedicating our mornings to time with God before diving into the digital world.

At first, I sometimes needed to have Caleb hide my phone. But over time, the habit of self-control transformed our mornings and set the tone for our entire day. We invite Jesus into every hour of our lives, relying on Him for self-control in every situation.

Caleb's steadfast commitment to this practice has shown me the power of discipline in shaping our lives, marriage, and ministry. Self-control is like a muscle; the more you use it, the stronger you become. We must rely on Jesus for strength and walk in step with the Holy Spirit for wisdom.

Self-control is not a restriction but a powerful tool that fortifies your marriage. Embrace it with patience, and watch your love grow deeper and more resilient.

Heavenly Father, thank You that self-control is a fruit of the Spirit. *As we live in You, You grow each of the fruits in us. I pray that You would help my husband practice self-control. Would You let it develop like a muscle as he uses it? Help him to understand that it is not merely a restraint from negative behaviors but a choice to love and respect each other deeply. May he prepare his mind for action that edifies our marriage and glorifies You. Would You nudge him to show discipline with the food he eats, the media he consumes, and all that he does?*

In moments of trial and temptation, grant us the wisdom and self-control to respond with godliness rather than react with impulsivity. Let self-control be the cornerstone of our love, keeping it disciplined and focused on Your will.

I pray for Your Holy Spirit to work in us, producing the fruit of self-control, which strengthens our marriage and reflects Your love to the world. Amen.

Let self-control guard your mornings, and you'll find God's presence throughout your day.

love in action . . .

Together: Establish a no-phone, God-first morning routine to strengthen your spiritual connection as a couple.

For him: Encourage your husband when you see him exercising self-control.

WEEK

28

RESTORED AND REDEEMED

A prayer for trusting God's timing

Take delight in the L*ORD*, *and he will give you your heart's desires. Commit everything you do to the* L*ORD*. *Trust him, and he will help you.*

PSALM 37:4-5

I had prayed all my life for a wonderful husband. When I got engaged, I thought my dreams were coming true. But my world crumbled when my fiancé ended our relationship.

Would I give up on God, feeling betrayed and abandoned, or would I continue to seek His will? God held me close during that season, using the heartbreak to show me where my true worth lay, teaching me to depend on Him for my happiness. He began to unravel and reshape the old relationship patterns.

In the City of Angels, God revealed His plan. I met Caleb, and our love story unfolded with a beauty that surpassed my dreams. God's timing was vastly different from mine, but His ways are always better. He used my pain to mold me and prepare me for an incredible love story.

On tough days in our marriage, I would sometimes forget that. My heart grew dull, and complaints crept in. But I realized how important it is to reflect on God's past faithfulness. He was faithful before, and He will be again.

In the hard seasons, God can restore and redeem us to even better than before. He can mend broken relationships, heal wounded hearts, and redeem impossible situations. Keep trusting, keep seeking, and know that God's plan is filled with hope and goodness.

Dear heavenly Father, Your plans are perfect. *Your ways and Your thoughts are higher than our thoughts. Sometimes from our perspective, we don't understand how You could make our longings work out. But God, I trust that You planted the desires of our hearts there for a reason. You have put the desires and dreams in my husband's heart, and You know them even better than he does himself. As he prays for specific hopes, help him to keep trusting Your plans and purpose for his life and our marriage. May he not lean on his own understanding, but in all ways acknowledge You. I know You will make his path straight.*

You've said in Your Word that when we delight in You, You will give us the desires of our hearts. Help my husband to seek Your heart and desire Your presence. Let him want this more than any gift. Let us not forget all the prayers You have answered in the past. May we talk about Your faithfulness often and recount Your goodness. I trust that You are working even difficult things for our good and for the good of Your Kingdom. Help my husband and me have this truth at the forefront of our minds. Amen.

God's plans are perfect, and His timing is impeccable. Keep trusting, keep seeking, and watch His goodness unfold.

love in action . . .

Together: Plan a special date night for sharing your dreams and aspirations. Pray for God's guidance in pursuing these dreams.

For him: Encourage your husband with ways you've seen God's faithfulness in answering prayers in his life.

WEEK

29

DEEP LONGINGS

A prayer for peace and contentment

True godliness with contentment is itself great wealth.

1 TIMOTHY 6:6

There's a deep longing in my heart to be a mother. It seemed like the best answer to prayer when after nine years of waiting, we finally learned we were pregnant with twins. But that dream was soon ripped from us when we lost our baby boys, Shiloh and Asher, to miscarriage.

The weight of that loss was heartbreaking enough, but it also gave birth to feelings of inadequacy. As I watched other families with children, my joy for them was genuine. But it was often followed by an uninvited guest: comparison. *Why do they have what I so desperately desire?*

Caleb's wise and loving words began to reshape my perspective. "I'm so full and content in my life with you, Stefanie," he said. "You are not a failure. You are more than enough for me. I'm so proud of you."

Together, we shifted our mindset to focus on our blessings, cherish the moments we share, and thank God for the journey designed specifically for us.

Comparison kills our joy and keeps us from experiencing contentment. But God cares deeply about filling our lives with good things. In the waiting, He will give us peace as we look to Him.

Heavenly Father, in the midst of our deepest unmet desires and unfulfilled dreams, I come before You seeking contentment. *I surrender the tendency to compare our journey with others, and instead, I embrace the uniqueness of the path You've laid out for us.*

Thank You for the gift of my husband. I pray against any urge he has to complain or let comparison set into his heart. Would You allow him to pour his heart out to You and choose gratitude and praise in all circumstances?

Lord, I lay before You the pain of our losses and disappointments, trusting that Your plans are greater than our understanding. Help us find contentment in the love we share, the moments we create, and the hope we have in You.

Please give us the strength to turn our hearts toward gratitude, even in the face of unmet desires. May our marriage be a testament to Your faithfulness as we find contentment in our unique journey. Help us find peace in our life with You. Fill every empty corner of our hearts with Your perfect presence. In Jesus' name, I pray. Amen.

Contentment blooms in the soil of gratitude. Embrace the unique journey God has designed for your marriage and find joy in His presence.

love in action . . .

Together: Write down three unique qualities of your marriage that set it apart from others. Celebrate these special aspects of your relationship.

For him: Tell your husband each day how full and content you are in your life and relationship with him.

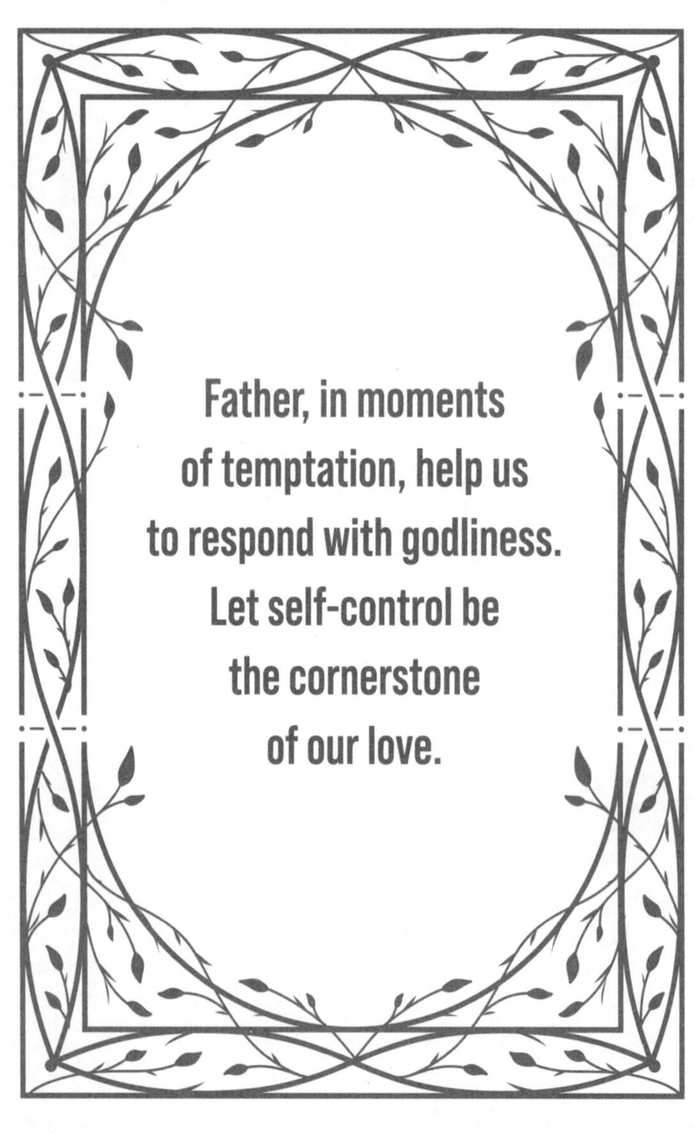

Father, in moments
of temptation, help us
to respond with godliness.
Let self-control be
the cornerstone
of our love.

WEEK

30

COMFORT IN WEAKNESS

A prayer for trusting God in trials

The Lord is close to the brokenhearted;
he rescues those whose spirits are crushed.

PSALM 34:18

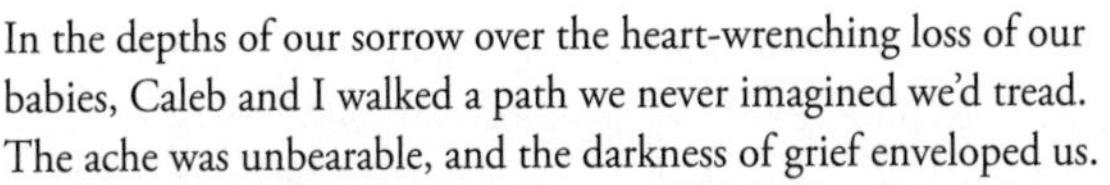

In the depths of our sorrow over the heart-wrenching loss of our babies, Caleb and I walked a path we never imagined we'd tread. The ache was unbearable, and the darkness of grief enveloped us.

During those long nights of tears and questioning, we clung to the promise that the Lord is close to the brokenhearted. An online follower from India wrote us a song based on this Scripture:

The Lord is close to the brokenhearted
and rescues those whose spirits are crushed.
Lord, bless their babies, Asher and Shiloh,
they're in Your safe hands, oh my dear Jesus.
God bless Stefanie and Caleb, Lord,
let them continue to honor You.
Even in these hard times, they are trusting You alone.
May You be their comfort.

The words still echo in my soul. We claimed these truths even when we didn't feel them. In our grief, we learned to trust God's presence more deeply. We poured out our hearts to Him and found comfort and strength in our weakest moments.

Over time, we have discovered that our pain could be a source of comfort to others. We share our story of loss, offering a listening ear and a shoulder to cry on to those who have walked a similar path.

Heavenly Father, in the midst of our trials and heartaches, I find peace in Your presence. *You are close to the brokenhearted, and I thank You for rescuing us when our spirits were crushed.*

Lord, help my husband to trust in Your promise that joy will come in the morning, even when he walks through the darkest valleys. Strengthen him, hold him up, and be his refuge in times of trouble.

I pray for any pain my husband is experiencing. Would You help him to draw close to You and be real about his emotions? Thank You for molding him to be even more like You during the trials he is enduring. Even in times of weakness, would You be his strength and help?

May our own experiences of pain become a source of comfort and hope to others. Use us to extend Your love and compassion to those who are hurting, just as You have comforted us. Thank You for Your presence and comfort. Amen.

Trust in the God who is close to the brokenhearted. Your pain can be a source of comfort to others, and joy will come soon.

love in action . . .

Together: In trials, seek God's guidance and comfort to strengthen your bond and gain unity.

For him: Take time to listen and validate your husband's feelings during difficult moments.

WEEK

31

CULTIVATING ROMANCE

A prayer for intimacy

Let your wife be a fountain of blessing for you. Rejoice in the wife of your youth. She is a loving deer, a graceful doe. Let her breasts satisfy you always. May you always be captivated by her love.

PROVERBS 5:18-19

In the busyness of life, it's easy to let the romance slip away in our marriage. But intimacy isn't cultivated only in the bedroom. The way you treat each other all day makes a big impact on your physical connection. Intentional words and actions can keep the flame burning bright.

I've made a habit of telling my husband how handsome he is throughout the day. Building him up and making him feel like my hero can make a world of difference. I remind him of his strength, his wisdom, and his character, boosting his confidence and making him feel desired. When he does something that makes me feel loved or appreciated, I make sure to let him know.

I'm a strong advocate of initiating intimacy as much as I can and never turning my husband down when he initiates, if at all possible. Being unselfish in the bedroom and communicating openly after our moments of intimacy cultivates a deeper connection between us.

Each couple is unique, and everyone has different preferences. It's important to learn about our spouse's needs and desires so we can love each other well. When we keep our husbands as the apple of our eye, we continue to nurture the intimacy and romance that make our marriage strong.

Dear Lord, thank You that You thought of the idea of two becoming one. *I pray You would keep the flame of intimacy burning in our marriage always. I pray our connection would only get better over time.*

Father, would You give my husband a deep passion for me? Would You allow his eyes to see me as beautifully and wonderfully made? Even as I age, I pray he finds me more beautiful because of our connection, and I pray I would feel the same about him. Help him to be selfless in the way he loves me. I pray that nothing would pollute his mind. Protect us both from anything that would steal our attention away from each other.

Thank You for the gift of intimacy. Help us to continually cultivate and cherish this special bond. Teach us to use our words and actions to build each other up and keep the romance alive throughout the day.

Lord, may we always be intoxicated by each other's love. If ever we feel the flame burning out, would You light it brightly again? Through the ebb and flow of marriage, protect us, guard us, and build us up stronger in love. Amen.

Keep the flame of intimacy burning with loving words and acts of affection.

love in action . . .

Together: Practice honest communication after moments of intimacy. Learn about each other's desires and preferences.

For him: Compliment your husband's appearance and character regularly. Initiate intimacy and prioritize physical connection.

WEEK

32

IGNITING DREAMS

A prayer for his career path

May the favor of the Lord our God rest on us; establish the work of our hands for us—yes, establish the work of our hands.

PSALM 90:17, NIV

When I married Caleb, he was a passionate teacher, pouring his energy and care into the lives of children. His gift was evident, but there was a restlessness beneath the surface. He could not shake his shattered dream of playing basketball.

I began to pray fervently for God to birth a new dream in my husband's heart. I encouraged Caleb, highlighting his incredible qualities and talents and urging him to seek God's guidance in healing past wounds and rediscovering his purpose.

When I began working online, Caleb supported me and took part. As he sacrificially loved me in my calling, something amazing happened. He started seeking God at a whole new level. New dreams sprouted within him about sharing the gospel online and inspiring healthy, God-honoring relationships. It breathed life and purpose into both of us.

As wives, we have great influence over our husbands. Building them up with our prayers and words has a tremendous impact. As we run after God and after the dreams He places on our hearts, it can also spark dreams in our husbands. Marriage is about more than the two of us. It's about impacting the Kingdom and being a light together. If that seems really far from you right now, don't give up hope. God is working through your prayers!

Dear heavenly Father, thank You that You are a God of purpose. *You created my husband, and You knew him before Creation. You planted dreams and passions in his heart, some of which You may have already revealed, and some of which may still be hidden. Would You help my husband seek You with all his heart? As he acknowledges You, would You make his path clear? Would You deeply heal any areas of pain and show him his identity and value in You?*

Please give my husband favor and respect among his colleagues, and may he shine brightly in his workplace, as an employee and a leader. Lord, help him find joy and purpose in the work he does, and if You ever lead him to a different path, may he trust Your perfect plan.

Would You also encourage me to keep seeking You and Your plan for my life? Help us to celebrate one another's gifts and not compare or be jealous. As I seek You and walk in my purpose, help this to inspire my husband to walk out his own purpose. Remind him that his true worth lies in his identity as Your child, and may his work flow from the abundance of love and purpose he finds in You. Amen.

Supporting your husband's dreams isn't just about worldly success. It's about building a marriage that thrives under God's guidance.

love in action . . .

Together: Celebrate each other's achievements, big and small, and let each other know how proud you are.

For him: Love your husband unconditionally, reminding him of his worth in God's eyes, regardless of achievements.

WEEK

33

REALIGNING PRIORITIES

A prayer for keeping God at the center

Search me, O God, and know my heart; test me and know my anxious thoughts. Point out anything in me that offends you, and lead me along the path of everlasting life.

PSALM 139:23-24

In my last year of teaching, I felt like I wasn't on God's path for me. I was restless and frustrated, and I told Caleb often about my disconnect. In turn, he struggled with feeling like a failure as a husband because I was so discontented.

We found ourselves spending more time than we should have on things that weren't leading to life, and we had misplaced priorities. Caleb immersed himself in video games, seeking escape from life's uncertainties. I was entangled in social media and Pinterest, comparing our lives to others and complaining about what we lacked. We were both discouraged, and judgment and criticism crept in.

I started my day in the Word but often failed to invite God into the other twenty-three hours. Unknowingly, I used my time in Scripture to bolster my sense of superiority over my husband regarding our priorities. But God began to work on our hearts, peeling away the layers of concealed pain.

As we genuinely sought God's guidance, our priorities underwent a transformation. Nagging and complaining had not changed anything, but God's love and our prayers did. We learned that speaking the truth kindly and compassionately was far more effective. I now regularly ask God to search our hearts and point out anything offensive, allowing Him to realign our priorities with His path.

Dear heavenly Father, thank You that You know us better than we know ourselves. *You created us and know what will be most fulfilling to our souls. If our priorities are off-center, please gently correct us.*

I thank You for my husband. If there is anything he is spending time on that isn't ultimately bringing life to him, others, and our marriage, would You convict him of this? Give him the determination and power to shift any priorities that aren't in line with Your will for him.

I'm sorry for the times I've been critical or judgmental of the way he spends his time. Would You help me to go to You first in prayer? If I need to address a concern with him, would You help me to do so with grace and compassion? Keep me from trying to get the speck out of his eye while I have a plank in my own—such as being judgmental or controlling.

Thank You that every day is a fresh start with You! Search and know our hearts. Take out anything You don't want to be there. Let us live twenty-four hours a day giving You access. Direct our paths, and let us seek Your Kingdom first. Amen.

Let God's love realign your priorities, and watch your marriage thrive.

love in action . . .

Together: Plan a picnic date, taking your Bibles along. Pray for God's nudging about priorities that need to be shifted.

For him: If you need to approach your husband about misplaced priorities, seek God's guidance and speak the truth in love.

WEEK

34

A SEA OF UNCERTAINTY

A prayer for keeping hope alive

Hope deferred makes the heart sick,
but a dream fulfilled is a tree of life.
PROVERBS 13:12

In our marriage, we have had moments when it seemed our hope was under siege. We felt directionless, lost in a sea of uncertainty, after facing attack and broken promises from others. I vividly remember how it broke my heart to see my husband's hopes dashed.

We drowned our disappointment in Pinterest, social media, and video games, seeking refuge from our feelings of failure and hopelessness. Using these distractions as a coping mechanism only prolonged our pain. We had allowed the world's standards to dictate our worth and happiness, and it left us empty. We had placed our hope in the wrong things.

But here's the beautiful truth: Christ's hope never fails. As we began to place our hope in God, He breathed new life into our marriage. We learned to allow His truth and love to minister to our pain.

As we brought our prayers to Him, He started fulfilling the desires of our hearts in ways we never thought possible. With new discouragements, we remind each other that God was faithful before and will be again. We no longer need to cope with our dashed hopes in ways that aren't bringing us life. He can help us see ourselves, others, and our circumstances with fresh eyes.

Dear heavenly Father, I come to You today with a grateful heart for Your unwavering hope that restores my husband and me, even in our darkest moments. *Lord, I confess the times I have placed my hope in things other than You, only to be left disappointed and empty. Thank You for Your forgiveness and guidance.*

Lord, I know hope deferred makes the heart sick, but a longing fulfilled is a tree of life. Would You breathe new hope into my husband's heart today? Would You encourage him in his identity in You? I pray that he would spend time with You and invite You into all he does throughout the day. Fill his heart with Your hope, O Lord, and renew his spirit. Help him to trust in Your plans, which are for his good and not for disaster. Strengthen him to place his hope in You alone, for You are the source of joy and peace.

May Your Word be our refuge and shield, providing the direction we need in our marriage. Let it breathe new life into our relationship, even in times of uncertainty. Thank You for planting new dreams and longings in our hearts, guiding us to a deeper hope that can only be found in You. Amen.

In God, our hope is unshakable and our love is unstoppable. Let Him breathe fresh hope into your marriage today.

love in action . . .

Together: When facing challenges, seek guidance from godly mentors. Let others speak hope into your life.

For him: If your husband is feeling hopeless in any way, pray for him and tell him how you see God's purpose at work in his life.

WEEK

35

LIGHT IN THE DARKNESS

A prayer for a heart of worship in all circumstances

I will praise the LORD at all times. I will constantly speak his praises. I will boast only in the LORD; let all who are helpless take heart. Come, let us tell of the LORD's greatness; let us exalt his name together.

PSALM 34:1-3

The day we found out that our babies were no longer alive in my womb, we were crushed beyond words. I looked at Caleb with wide eyes and tears flowing down. My voice trembling with grief and shock, I asked, "What are we going to do?"

Caleb, with a calm determination, responded, "We are going to worship God."

His words pierced through the darkness of despair like a ray of light, so sitting on the couch, we put on worship songs, and their melodies filled the air. Hillsong's "Highlands (Song of Ascent)" was especially fitting:

I will praise You on the mountain
And I will praise You when the mountain's in my way . . .
No less God within the shadows . . .
In the highlands and the heartache all the same.[3]

Tears streamed down our faces as we sang with all our hearts, our hands reaching upward like children longing to be held by their heavenly Father. Caleb's words echoed in my mind: "He is worthy of our worship in our best moments and our worst moments." This became the anthem of our grief, a lifeline when our hearts are heavy with sorrow. In worship, we find the inexplicable peace that only God's presence can bring.

---

3 Hillsong UNITED, "Highlands (Song of Ascent)," by Benjamin William Hastings and Joel Timothy Houston, recorded April 26, 2019, track 8 on *People (Live)*, Capitol Christian Music Group, Inc.

Heavenly Father, thank You for Your constant presence. *You are worthy of our worship in every circumstance. Thank You for the strength and comfort You provide, especially during our deepest sorrow and loss.*

I pray that You would make my husband a passionate worshiper of You, with his songs but also with his actions throughout the day. If there is any hardness in his heart toward You, would You heal it? Pursue him and let others encourage him and point him to Your goodness. I pray that we can be a couple that worships You together with all our hearts and souls and strength.

Help us, Lord, to remember that worship is equally essential in our worst moments. Your presence brings peace that surpasses understanding. Let worship be the anchor that keeps our hearts tethered to You, even in the storms of life. Amen.

Worship God at all times, for He is worthy in every moment.

love in action . . .

Together: Attend a worship service or conference to experience corporate worship as a couple.

For him: Make worship a regular part of your daily routine. Let the peace of God's presence flow from you to bless your husband.

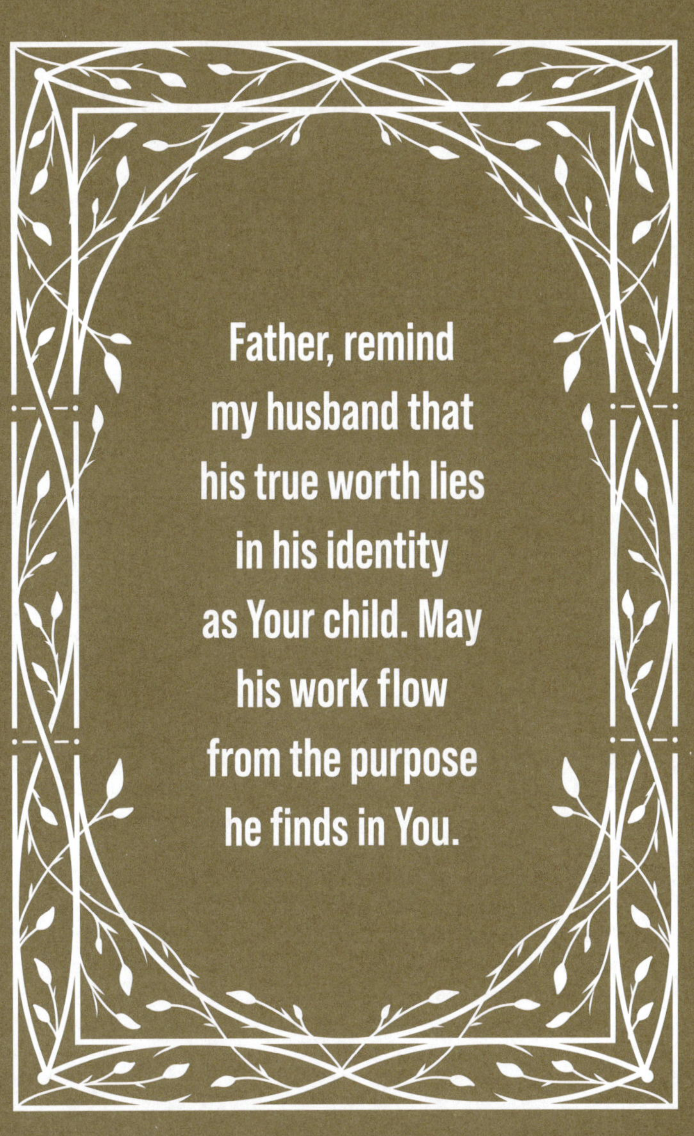

Father, remind
my husband that
his true worth lies
in his identity
as Your child. May
his work flow
from the purpose
he finds in You.

WEEK

36

CHERISH EVERY MOMENT

A prayer for companionship

Two people are better off than one, for they can help each other succeed. If one person falls, the other can reach out and help. But someone who falls alone is in real trouble.

ECCLESIASTES 4:9-10

My relationship with Caleb was built upon friendship. In the weeks before our first date, we spent hours in group hangouts with friends, sharing laughter, stories, and unforgettable moments.

Our first date was a testament to the power of companionship. Over a delicious meal, we engaged in deep conversation, our laughter filling the air. Afterward, we enjoyed frozen yogurt and strolled through the streets of Pasadena. We couldn't get enough of each other, and we sat on a bench near city hall, feeling safe and deeply seen until two in the morning. We reveled in each other's presence and relished the simple joy of companionship.

Now, whether we are belting out tunes during car-karaoke sessions, spontaneously breaking into dance parties at home, composing silly songs, or simply embracing each other in laughter, we try to cherish every moment. We thrive on planning adventures, indulging in board games, sharing time with family and friends, and cuddling with our beloved pets to watch good shows.

Our secret? Intentionality. We don't always get it right, but we consciously choose to take an interest in each other's passions and to create a safe space for growth and authenticity. Companionship with your husband is a priceless gift, one that will become more precious as you make time to be there for each other.

Heavenly Father, thank You for being the best companion. *Help us to take delight in Your company. Help us to invite You into every moment of our day.*

I thank You for my husband. Would You help him to cherish time with me? May he delight in my company and be intentional about cultivating a better friendship with me. I pray that You will continue to strengthen our bond, reminding us of the importance of friendship within our marriage. Help us, Lord, to be intentional in our companionship. May we always take a genuine interest in each other's passions and dreams, supporting one another in this journey.

Give us wisdom to create a safe space where we can be vulnerable and be our authentic selves without fear of judgment. Teach us to cherish the moments we share, from fun activities to quiet nights at home, for every moment is a gift from You. Let us delight in the unique way You've made both of us. Let offense and pain be healed so our love grows. May You continue to be the glue our marriage needs. Amen.

Companionship is about synchronizing your steps, finding balance, and enjoying the dance side by side.

love in action . . .

Together: Engage in activities you both enjoy. Share a hobby, a sport, or a favorite show.

For him: Learn more about your husband's interests and passions. Ask questions and show genuine curiosity.

WEEK

37

THE EXTRAORDINARILY ORDINARY

A prayer for lighthearted joy

A glad heart makes a happy face; a broken heart crushes the spirit.

PROVERBS 15:13

It was our third year of marriage, and life's burdens bore down on us like a storm cloud. Yet, in the midst of it all, we stumbled upon a moment that taught us the profound beauty of lighthearted joy.

One evening, hearts heavy and frustrations palpable, we went to the cinema with Caleb's mom, Kay, and his dad, John. The enchanting world of *Cinderella*, in its 2015 rendition, was a brief escape from our worries. After the credits rolled, something magical happened.

As we exited the theater, moonlight bathed the parking lot in a soft glow. Spontaneously, Kay and I began to sing "Lavender's Blue" from the movie. John and Caleb put on the headlights of our cars, then grabbed our hands. Momma Kay and Poppa John danced in the moonlit space, and Caleb twirled me around and around.

It felt as though the weight of the world was gone, and our hearts were light as feathers. It was a moment of pure, unbridled joy that etched itself into our souls. It was a Hallmark moment, and we try to cultivate many more just like it.

There is beauty in ordinary moments if we look for it. Even in life's most trying days, there is room for laughter, for spontaneity, and for the kind of joy that transcends circumstance.

Dear heavenly Father, You created joy and laughter. *Would You bless our marriage with more of this wonderful gift? My husband often holds the burdens of our family concerns on his shoulders. Would You help him to take deep breaths and place his burdens all on You? Give him the humility and grace to enjoy little moments more. Help him to embrace spontaneous moments without taking things too seriously. Even when we are dealing with pain, loss, and stress, would You help us to be intentional about finding glimpses of joy?*

We know there's a season and time for everything, a time to laugh, a time to cry, and a time to dance. Help us not to be too caught up in the mundane to miss the extraordinarily ordinary moments. Let us drop any pretension or pride that could keep us from embracing Your abundant joy.

Help us create beautiful memories that strengthen our bond as a couple and as a family. Fill our hearts with laughter, love, and deep appreciation for the small, joyful moments that bring light into our lives. May our marriage be a testament to the joy and healing that come from Your presence. Amen.

Moments of lighthearted joy can bring powerful healing. Embrace laughter, create memories, and let love shine.

love in action . . .

Together: Be deliberate about creating lighthearted moments in your marriage, especially during challenging times.

For him: Let go of routines and allow spontaneity to lead to unexpected adventures and joy that will bless your husband.

WEEK

38

A BREEZE IN THE STORM

A prayer for renewal

Restore us, O Lord, and bring us back to you again! Give us back the joys we once had!

LAMENTATIONS 5:21

After three grueling years, our dream of working together had become a reality. Caleb had finally been able to leave his teaching job and join me full-time. But this dream was very soon tested as the world around us unraveled and an unexpected storm entered our lives.

It was a year of uncertainty, and our dreams appeared to hang by a thread. All our sources of business revenue were on hold because of the pandemic. On top of that, our car was stolen. It felt like a punch in the gut.

Caleb and I sought God like never before. We spent hours reading His Word. We went on long walks and prayed. In those moments, we realized something extraordinary was happening. God was using this season to renew us in ways we hadn't anticipated. He unearthed hidden issues in us—issues we hadn't even known needed addressing.

Through prayer and reflection, we allowed God's renewing power to flow over us. Like a gentle breeze in the midst of a storm, His presence swept away the debris of doubt and fear, revealing a path forward. In surrender, we found rejuvenation not only in our faith but also in our marriage. In the stolen moments of 2020, God transformed our hearts, revealing that even amid uncertainty, renewal and restoration are possible through His grace and love.

Heavenly Father, thank You that You are in the business of renewal. *You restore dead dreams. You create new things even from bad circumstances. I thank You for my husband. In areas in which he has experienced loss or in which his dreams have been hindered, would You revive his spirit once again? Help him to recognize his need for revitalization. Your Word reminds us that our spirits can be renewed each day, even when our bodies are weak. I humbly seek that renewal now.*

Father, create in my husband a clean heart, and remove any impurities, doubts, or negativity that may have taken root within him. Renew in him a steadfast and loyal spirit, fully devoted to You. Restore us, O Lord, to the joy and fervor we once had in our relationship with You and each other. May Your love renew our souls, and may we find comfort in Your embrace. Amen.

In every storm, God can bring restoration. Our setbacks can be stepping stones to a renewed purpose.

love in action . . .

Together: During dinner or a walk, reflect on how God has renewed your faith during challenging times.

For him: Pray and seek God's renewal in your husband's life, your own life, and your marriage.

WEEK

39

EMBRACE THE UNKNOWN

A prayer for fearless adventure

He will order his angels to protect you wherever you go. They will hold you up with their hands so you won't even hurt your foot on a stone. You will trample upon lions and cobras; you will crush fierce lions and serpents under your feet!

PSALM 91:11-13

By the fall of 2020, my heart longed to reunite with family in Pittsburgh, Pennsylvania. But fear gripped me. The idea of flying during a pandemic was daunting, but my longing was undeniable. So, Caleb and I embarked on an audacious adventure—a cross-country road trip.

As we set out from sunny Pasadena, anxiety gripped me tightly, and I clung to Psalm 91 as a lifeline, praying it every day. We journeyed through many landscapes, visiting awe-inspiring national parks along the way. At first, though, my fears kept me from truly enjoying the beauty.

But then something miraculous occurred. We spent the second night at Bryce Canyon in Utah, where we joined a stargazing walk. As I looked up at the vast, starry sky, my anxiety dissipated. The brilliance of God's stars above, the beauty of His infinite creation, and the knowledge of His boundless love overwhelmed me. I realized that God's handiwork was everywhere, even in the midst of uncertainty.

Sometimes we must confront our fears head-on to experience the joy of adventure. As wives, let us embrace the unknown, for in the adventure of marriage, we discover the depth of His love.

Dear heavenly Father, You created the heavens and the earth. *Nothing is impossible for You. In the midst of uncertainty, You are still the peace that supports our marriage. Thank You for guiding my husband and me through life's adventures, even when anxiety threatens to paralyze us. When my husband faces those moments of fear, I pray that he would have eyes to see the beauty of Your creation and remember that it was Your powerful hand that made it. May that knowledge overcome his anxiety and help him to enjoy the times we have together.*

Would You also place on his heart a desire to take adventures with me and even create moments of adventure in our everyday life? Lord, I pray I can be a more fun and adventurous wife too. Let me cast my fears on You as I embrace the beauty You have in store for me and my husband. Give us wisdom and protection, and help us to know we are covered in Your love. May we learn to cast aside anxiety and fully enjoy the wonders of Your creation. Bless our marriage with a spirit of adventure, and may we grow closer as we explore the world together. Amen.

In the adventure of marriage, fear may try to be a passenger, but let God do the driving. Trust His protection and embrace the unknown together.

love in action . . .

Together: Hold hands and look up at the stars together. Let the vastness of the sky remind you of God's boundless love and protection.

For him: Suggest an activity that would allow you and your husband to experience God's creation.

WEEK

40

BIRTHING NEW DREAMS

A prayer for shared purpose

Make me truly happy by agreeing wholeheartedly with each other, loving one another, and working together with one mind and purpose.

PHILIPPIANS 2:2

In a marriage, two unique souls come together, each with their own dreams and visions. Caleb and I embarked on this adventure with our individual aspirations, unaware of the extraordinary mutual goals God had in store for us.

God ignited a shared vision within us—to spread the gospel and encourage people in their marriage and relationships—but we quickly realized we didn't have it all figured out. God has continually redirected us, refined us, and aligned our hearts with His purpose.

Marriage is designed to be a living testament to God's goodness. This doesn't mean you have to work full-time together in ministry. You could minister by leading your family in Bible study, organizing a prayer walk around your neighborhood, or coaching a sport together to impact the next generation. Maybe you have the gift of blessing ministries financially, or maybe the gift of prayer. Perhaps you can help lead a retreat or make a meal for a hurting neighbor.

When your individual gifts come together, it can impact the Kingdom for eternity. Doing something with a shared purpose and vision will unite you and be a blessing this world needs.

Heavenly Father, thank You for putting dreams, vision, and purpose in our hearts. *I pray for unity of vision in our marriage. It's not an accident that my husband and I are together. You knew how our union could impact Your Kingdom for eternity. Would You ignite the dreams You have for us? Would You give us creative ideas about what we can do together for Your bigger purpose?*

Thank You for the way You've uniquely made my husband. Help me to build him up in the way You've made him. Let me be an asset to him and the goals You've given him, and let him do the same for me. Help us trust You and seek You humbly as we pursue these mutual goals. In moments of redirection and refinement, give us the wisdom to follow Your lead and the humility to submit to Your will. May our marriage be a testament to Your love and grace, a beacon of hope for our families and the world. Amen.

In seasons of change, allow God to birth new visions and dreams for your marriage.

love in action . . .

Together: Schedule a coffee date and ask God how He wants to use your combined gifts to impact the world.

For him: Encourage your husband about ways you see his gifts being able to impact the Kingdom.

WEEK

41

A BEACON IN THE DARKNESS

A prayer for generosity

The generous will prosper; those who refresh others will themselves be refreshed.

PROVERBS 11:25

There was a season when financial strain threatened to crush our dreams. The weight of unpaid bills and looming uncertainties pressed down on us relentlessly. It was during this challenging time that we experienced an act of generosity that would forever change our perspective on love, family, and the miraculous provision of God.

In the midst of our turmoil, a family member stepped forward with a gift like a lifeline. Their selfless act of kindness not only provided a temporary reprieve from our shortfall but also reawakened hope within our hearts. More than a mere financial transaction, this gift was an outpouring of love and compassion that affirmed our worth and purpose.

This extraordinary act of generosity served as a profound reminder that we were not alone in our struggles. It gave testimony to the boundless capacity for love within the bonds of family. The impact of that gift reverberated far beyond the relief it offered. It became a symbol of hope, a beacon in our darkest hour, and a source of inspiration for years to come. It allowed us to continue fulfilling the dream God had placed on our hearts. And it ignited in us a desire to be generous toward others even when it doesn't make sense.

Sometimes we get to be the ones extending generosity. At other times, we can receive it humbly and gratefully.

Heavenly Father, thank You for being so generous with us. *Every good gift comes from You. Thank You for Your provision. God, I pray that my husband would be generous to others out of the gifts You've given him. Help him to be able to receive generosity with gratitude and humility. And help him give to me and others out of the abundance of Your love.*

Lord, would You bless our marriage with generosity? Help us to know that we can never outgive You. Let us show generosity not to get something in return but to show our love and gratitude for You.

Teach us to be channels of Your blessing to others, just as we have been blessed. Help us to see opportunities for giving generously and selflessly, not just with our finances but with our time, love, and resources. Give us the wisdom to recognize when someone around us is in need, and give us the courage to step forward and make a difference. Let the spirit of generosity flow through our marriage. Amen.

Generosity is not just about *what* we give but *how* we give. May we bless others, just as we have been blessed.

love in action . . .

Together: Identify ways to be more generous as a couple, whether through giving, volunteering, or supporting a cause.

For him: Encourage your husband with a story about a time someone's generosity impacted your life.

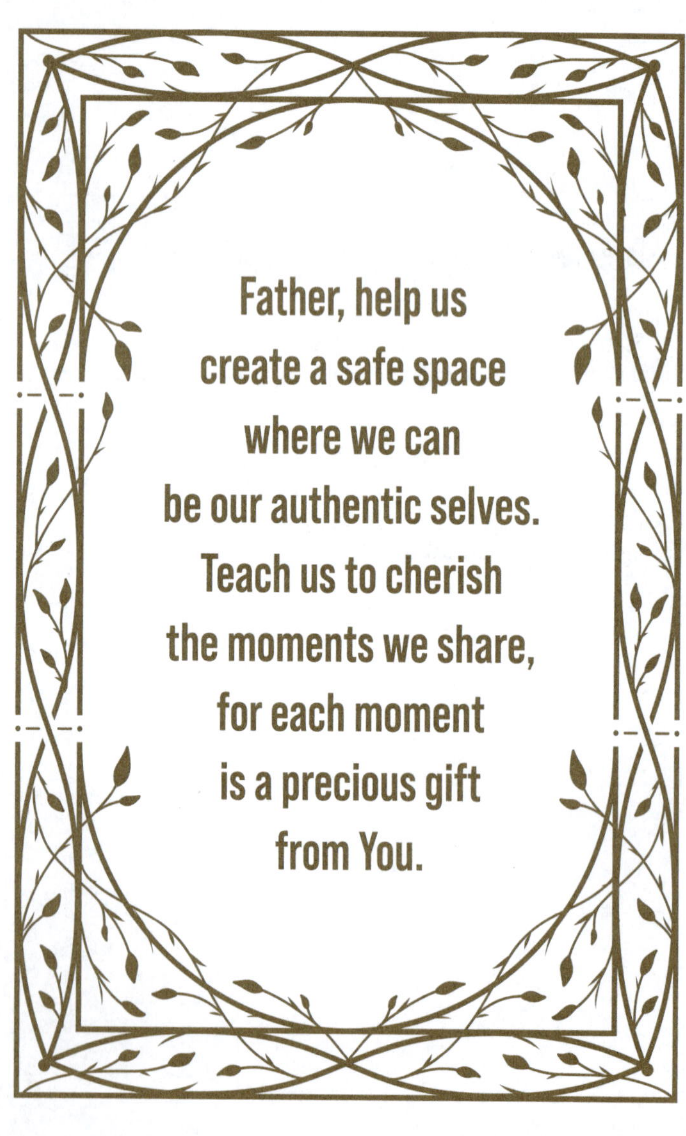

Father, help us
create a safe space
where we can
be our authentic selves.
Teach us to cherish
the moments we share,
for each moment
is a precious gift
from You.

WEEK

42

SAFE SPACE

A prayer for open communication

The heart of the righteous weighs its answers,
but the mouth of the wicked gushes evil.
PROVERBS 15:28, NIV

"Can you get this price tag off my shirt, my love?" I said to Caleb. It was our first year of marriage, and I was trying on a sweater Caleb had bought me. It was cute, and I wanted to wear it right away.

Caleb carefully removed the tag, but then I realized part of the plastic was still there. I blurted out, "Did you get the little back piece? It's the most annoying thing to have it jab me!"

Instead of fessing up, Caleb got creative. He held his middle finger against his thumb, pretending to have the piece in his hand. Arm outstretched, he dramatically opened his fingers over the trash can.

"Caleb, you're lying about finding the tag," I said, half-amused and half-mad at how absurdly obvious it was. He tried to deny it, but the jig was up. To this day, we both occasionally reach out our fingers and click our tongue, remembering that funny moment.

That first year of marriage taught us a valuable lesson about honesty and communication. We've both discovered that it's much more peaceful not to get worked up over little things that don't matter. This allows us to be honest even in situations that could potentially cause conflict.

A little humor and understanding can go a long way in building a stronger, more honest, and more peaceful marriage.

Heavenly Father, You are worthy of all our worship and praise.
Thank You that You are always honest and trustworthy. You call us to be like You. I pray that my husband would always have the courage to be honest with me and with You. I pray there wouldn't be any secrets between us. Help us to keep building trust and safety every day.

Give us wisdom to create an atmosphere of grace and peace where honesty can thrive. May our interactions be marked by openness and truthfulness, even when it may be challenging. I pray for the courage to admit our mistakes and the humility to accept honesty from each other. I confess there are times I haven't been fully honest with You and my husband. God, I thank You for Your forgiveness. Would You help me to be honest with myself, You, and my spouse? Let our love be a safe haven for transparency, free from judgment and condemnation. Amen.

Honesty creates a foundation of trust and understanding. Let love and grace pave the way to a peaceful relationship.

love in action . . .

Together: Practice being more vulnerable and open with each other.

For him: Extend grace to your husband, allowing for honesty without fear of judgment or conflict.

WEEK

43

SECRET JOKES AND SILLY SONGS

A prayer for cultivating laughter

A cheerful heart is good medicine,
but a crushed spirit dries up the bones.
PROVERBS 17:22, NIV

From the very beginning of our relationship, Caleb's humor has been like sunshine on a rainy day, bringing warmth and light to even the darkest moments. I remember the first time we sat down to dinner with friends. His jokes had me giggling uncontrollably. And when I mentioned my love for animals, he teased about them setting up camp in my hair! I laughed so hard, I thought I might snort.

Laughter has become something that continually bonds us. We have our own secret jokes, silly songs, and goofy dances that never fail to make us smile. Caleb's knack for defusing tension with a well-timed joke is a gift. Not every moment is a time for laughter, but the more I allow it in, the more blessed my life and marriage are. We've learned what makes each other laugh, and we've learned how to be honoring to each other and those around us even in our jokes. We never use laughter as a way to put anyone down. Instead, it's a way to uplift our home with joy.

Laughter is a balm for the soul. It lightens our burdens, lifts our spirits, and reminds us to cherish the simple joys of life. I encourage you to embrace the laughter in your marriage. Find those moments of silliness and joy, and let them fill your home with belly laughs and love. For in the end, it's the laughter that we'll remember most fondly—the moments when we let go of our worries and simply enjoy each other's company. Pause, breathe, and share as many laughs with your spouse as you can. You'll be amazed at how much brighter life becomes.

Heavenly Father, thank You for the gift of laughter and the joy it brings to our lives. *Help my husband and me to cultivate a spirit of humor in our marriage, finding moments of lightheartedness even in the midst of challenge. Give us Your wisdom for the right timing. Teach us to use humor to uplift each other and strengthen our bond, and give us the wisdom to know when it's appropriate to lighten the mood. Let us always honor each other and those around us in the way we joke. Help me to find my husband's jokes funny, and let us not take every moment too seriously to miss an opportunity to be silly or laugh. Let our marriage be a beacon of joy and laughter, reflecting Your love and grace to those around us. Amen.*

With every laugh shared, you deepen your connection with your husband.

love in action . . .

Together: Incorporate humor into your daily interactions, whether it's through playful banter, silly antics, or funny memes or videos.

For him: Share a joke or funny story with your husband today to lighten the mood and bring a smile to his face.

WEEK

44

RESCUE MISSION

A prayer for a compassionate heart

Since God chose you to be the holy people he loves, you must clothe yourselves with tenderhearted mercy, kindness, humility, gentleness, and patience.

COLOSSIANS 3:12

During a family trip to Minnesota, we embarked on a hike to a stunning waterfall. As the day unfolded, we went swimming in a serene pool of water. The steps back to our car were slippery and wet, and I fell hard, pulling back my big toenail and scraping my knee. I cried out in pain.

Caleb came to my rescue. He swiftly picked me up and, along with his dad, rushed me to the car. Caleb gently patted my head in comfort, while his dad bandaged my wounds. We had a big hiking trip planned for a few days later in Banff, Canada, and Caleb did so much to help me heal before the hike. He was so encouraging on the hike that even with my pain, we made it to our destination.

This act of compassion wasn't an isolated incident. Over the years, when I've been hurt, sick, or facing challenges, Caleb's unwavering compassion has been an incredible gift. His caring nature and ability to provide comfort have been a pillar of support.

However, like any couple, we've also faced times when we needed even deeper understanding. Occasionally, a past pain is triggered, causing us to act unkindly toward each other. It's a beautiful gift to respond even to snappiness with compassion, knowing the words are coming from a place of pain.

Heavenly Father, You are the source of all compassion, and I come before You in awe of Your goodness. *Thank You for Your unwavering love and grace. Your compassion is a testament to Your character, and I thank You that You are the God who sees us. Lord, You call us to reflect Your compassionate nature. I humbly confess that I sometimes fall short of this calling, both in my relationship with You and with my husband. I am grateful for Your forgiveness and grace.*

I want to express my gratitude for my husband. Would You increase his compassion, Lord? Would You give him eyes to see and a heart to understand when I face pain? Help him know how to comfort and soothe me. Would You also give me compassion for my husband? Let me see the best in him and long to understand him. Even in times that either of us acts out in pain, give us the grace to extend compassion. Amen.

Compassion is a beautiful gift. Nurture this quality in times of need, and watch your love flourish.

love in action . . .

Together: Be intentional about developing compassion in your relationship. Listen, offer a loving touch, and speak kind words.

For him: When your husband acts out in frustration or pain, look beyond the surface and extend grace and compassion.

WEEK

45

SUPERPOWER

A prayer for sensitivity

Gracious words are a honeycomb,
sweet to the soul and healing to the bones.
PROVERBS 16:24, NIV

Throughout my life, I've been labeled as "sensitive." Even when I was a child, the slightest look of disapproval or a particular tone of voice could bring tears to my eyes. I struggled to cope with the intensity of my emotions.

When I experienced betrayal from my first real boyfriend, it shattered my sensitive heart. I closed off a part of myself, and I embraced damaging beliefs such as *Guys don't have feelings* and *It's my turn to use guys.*

But God convicted me that men also possess emotions, even if they express them differently. I learned to manage my emotions more effectively, and God helped me to see my sensitivity as a superpower. I can be a healing light to others as God's love flows out of me in compassion. Caleb is often so grateful for the way I care for him out of this gift.

Yet, my sensitivity still surfaces in a negative way at times. It's been a significant learning curve discovering how to navigate this aspect of my personality. Speaking gently and kindly has a profound impact on our marriage. My husband is also sweet and sensitive, though in a different way. I love learning more about him and long to love him more every day. Learning to love each other sensitively helps our marriage thrive.

Heavenly Father, I bow before You because You are so good. *Thank You for being so faithful and compassionate and kind to us. Like me, my husband is filled with feelings and thoughts. Would You help him to reflect Your truth and love in those emotions? Would You give him the sensitivity to speak to me kindly? Increase his patience for me, and help him extend a loving embrace when needed. In times that he is feeling overwhelmed, would You help him process his emotions in a healthy way?*

I desire to be a wife who is caring and loving to my husband. Would You guard my verbal and nonverbal communication with my husband? Gentle my touch and soothe my tone of voice so I can reflect Your love to him. I pray that You would give us both the eyes and hearts to be gentle and sensitive toward each other. Let our words be sweet like honey. Amen.

Being sensitive to your husband's needs is a great gift to him. Taking things less personally will help your marriage thrive.

love in action . . .

Together: Talk about how well you empathize with each other's emotions. Share kindly about adjustments that could be helpful moving forward.

For him: Learn to let your sensitivity be a superpower in your interactions. Seek to understand your husband's feelings and reflect gentleness.

WEEK

46

24-7 CONNECTION

A prayer for a shared faith journey

Don't worry about anything; instead, pray about everything. Tell God what you need, and thank him for all he has done. Then you will experience God's peace, which exceeds anything we can understand. His peace will guard your hearts and minds as you live in Christ Jesus.

PHILIPPIANS 4:6-7

When we were first married, I often asked Caleb to pray for me. However, Caleb didn't feel as comfortable praying out loud as I did. But I continued inviting him to pray with me. I sometimes wish I had been more patient with his spiritual journey, but I don't regret any of those moments we shared in prayer.

My deepest desire was for both of us to hunger for 24-7 communication with God and to extend the love of Christ to those we encountered daily. I began to pray not only for our individual growth in prayer but also for our shared journey of faith. It's awe-inspiring to witness how God answered those prayers over time.

Caleb's transformation has been incredible. His life radiates his deep love for God, and he confidently prays in any circumstance. It has been a beautiful evolution. The way God has answered our prayers has even led us to write several books on prayer.

Throughout this journey, I've learned not to give up on prayer. Our marriage is a testament to prayer's transformative power. Those around us desperately need to hear about the boundless love of Jesus, and our marriage is a conduit for this message. Seeing Caleb's prayer life and the way he shares his faith now continually sharpens me in ways I'm so grateful for.

Heavenly Father, thank You that we can talk to You, the God who created the universe. *You placed all the stars in the sky. You made the seas and everything in them. Yet You invite us to talk to You, and You desire to communicate with us.*

Thank You that You created my husband and me to have fellowship with You and to share Your love with the world. Please increase my husband's hunger for You. Let him desire to talk to You first and foremost. Let him check in with You and listen to You throughout his day. May Your love pour out of him to me and to others.

I pray that our prayer life as a couple would grow each day. Help me to be a patient wife, but let me never give up on praying for my husband and for our marriage. I am thankful that You are the God of the impossible. You move in ways that are beyond our understanding. Lord, open our hearts to share our faith boldly. Amen.

Prayer has the power to enrich your marriage, and sharing your faith with others strengthens the bond between you.

love in action . . .

Together: Explore resources on prayer and faith-sharing to enrich your spiritual journey.

For him: Encourage your husband by reminding him that you pray for him every day.

WEEK

47

A SAFE HAVEN

A prayer for protection and unconditional love

Those who live in the shelter of the Most High will find rest in the shadow of the Almighty. This I declare about the LORD: He alone is my refuge, my place of safety; he is my God, and I trust him.

PSALM 91:1-2

As a young, single woman living in Los Angeles, I was eager to explore all the opportunities the bustling city had to offer. Hiking in the beautiful mountains became one of my favorite pastimes. But sometimes, I got a late start after classes, so my hikes would stretch past sunset.

When Caleb, known for his lighthearted nature, learned about my habit of hiking alone at night, he became serious. He made it clear that my well-being was his top priority. From that moment, I knew I had found someone who would go to great lengths to ensure my safety.

For instance, I had a friend's birthday party to attend in the city, and without hesitation, Caleb offered to drive me. He set up his workspace in a nearby coffee shop to wait, ensuring I wouldn't have to walk to my car alone after the event. He has consistently gone above and beyond to provide a sense of security for me.

Beyond physical safety, we also strive to create a secure space for each other within our relationship. We strive to offer unwavering support, empathize with one another, maintain consistency, respect each other's boundaries, and engage in open and honest communication. These actions contribute to a marriage filled with safety, trust, and love. God continually creates a haven of trust and security, where His grace guides our journey.

Heavenly Father, thank You that in You we can lie down in peace and sleep, and You will keep us safe. *You are our safe place. Even when we don't feel safe anywhere else, we can be safe in Your presence. Lord, help my husband find his security in You and not in the eyes of others. Please give him the guidance and wisdom to make our home safe and secure—physically, mentally, emotionally, and spiritually.*

For anything we've allowed into our hearts or lives that isn't proving to be safe, help us to create the right boundaries. Protect my husband and our marriage. Keep us in the shadow of Your wing. Help us to feel the security that comes from knowing You are guarding us as we walk with You. Help me to acknowledge the ways my husband looks out for me. Give me eyes to see the big and small ways he works to protect me and my relationship with him and You. Help us to keep growing in this area, and give us both grace as we are learning.

I pray that our marriage would help others around us feel safe and that our home would be an inviting place, radiating Your presence and peace to our friends and family. Amen.

When we honor and support one another, we create a haven of trust and security, where God's grace guides our journey.

love in action . . .

Together: Commit to fostering a relationship of trust and protection to enhance safety and security in your marriage.

For him: Ask God to help you see ways your husband looks out for you. Thank your husband for his care.

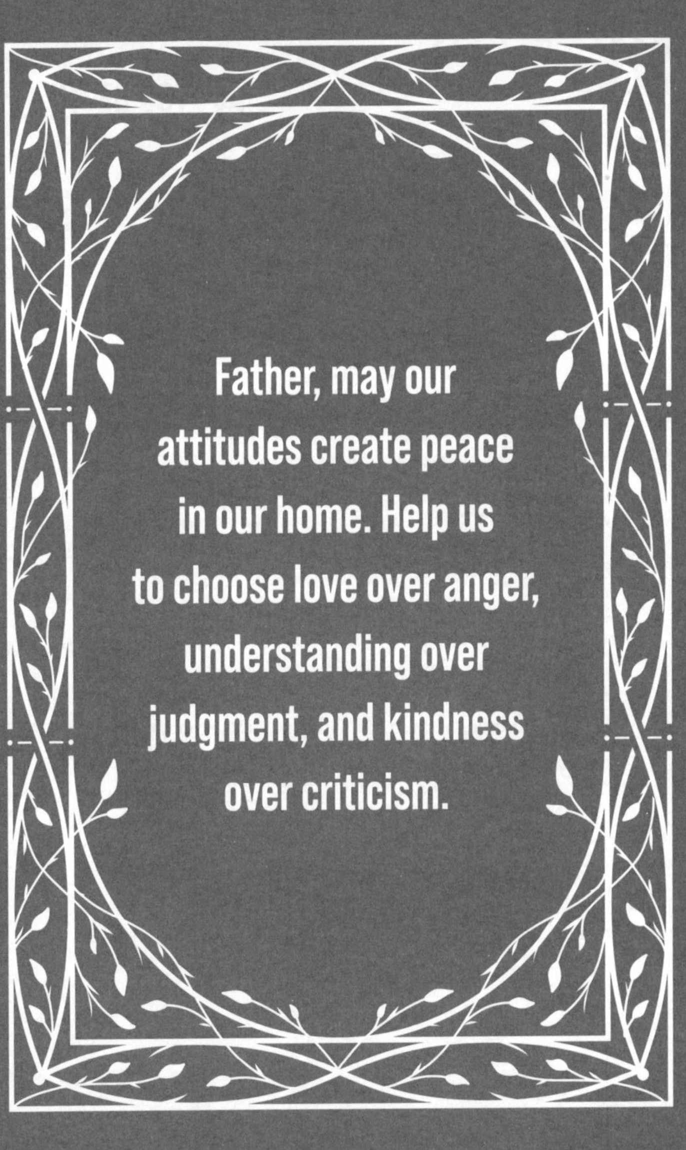

Father, may our attitudes create peace in our home. Help us to choose love over anger, understanding over judgment, and kindness over criticism.

WEEK

48

"TAG—YOU'RE IT!"

A prayer for a good attitude

The Holy Spirit produces this kind of fruit in our lives: love, joy, peace, patience, kindness, goodness, faithfulness, gentleness, and self-control.

GALATIANS 5:22-23

After working together for over a decade, Caleb and I realized that our moods could easily affect each other. If one of us entered the room with frustration or negativity, it had a ripple effect.

Instead of allowing our emotions to control us, we decided to take responsibility for our own feelings. We learned to be mindful of how our attitudes influenced the dynamics in our marriage. We took breaks when our interactions turned sour, asking God to restore peace and kindness.

Once, on a work trip to Saint Louis, I was in a particularly bad frame of mind, but Caleb kept doing what he could to encourage me. Even at Forest Park, in the midst of its beauty, I still couldn't shake my bad mood. But all of a sudden, I just decided to have fun.

"Tag—you're it!" I said, tapping Caleb on the shoulder. I ran up the big grassy hill with him close behind. He spun me around, and we laughed and laughed. It's a moment chiseled in both of our hearts.

We can't control each other's emotions, but we can choose how we respond. When we offer our frustrations to God and take accountability for our influence on each other, it transforms our marriage.

Heavenly Father, thank You for the gift of marriage and the opportunity to grow together in love and unity. *Help us to cultivate positive attitudes, kindness, and goodness in our marriage. Teach us to be mindful of how our words and actions affect each other. When frustration or negativity creeps in, may Your Holy Spirit prompt us to seek Your guidance and take a step back if needed.*

Give my husband strength to see the best in me. And give me eyes to see the best in him. I pray we would both have the willingness to encourage and uplift each other daily. May our words be seasoned with kindness, and may our actions reflect the goodness of Your love.

As we navigate the ups and downs of married life, may our attitudes create an atmosphere of peace and positivity in our home. Help us to choose love over anger, understanding over judgment, and kindness over criticism. In the name of Jesus, who exemplified perfect kindness and goodness, I pray. Amen.

When we choose kindness and goodness, we create an atmosphere of love and positivity that reflects God's grace.

love in action . . .

Together: Agree to each take accountability for your own actions and to strive for an atmosphere of kindness and goodness.

For him: Reflect on the impact of your attitude on your husband. Commit to encouraging your husband with kind words.

WEEK

49

CHAMPION OF MY HEART

A prayer that he feels appreciated

Love is patient and kind. Love is not jealous or boastful or proud or rude. It does not demand its own way. It is not irritable, and it keeps no record of being wronged. It does not rejoice about injustice but rejoices whenever the truth wins out. Love never gives up, never loses faith, is always hopeful, and endures through every circumstance.

1 CORINTHIANS 13:4-7

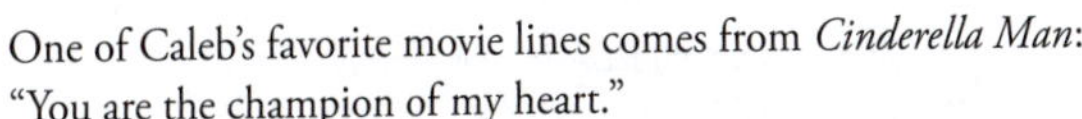

One of Caleb's favorite movie lines comes from *Cinderella Man*: "You are the champion of my heart."

It stirred deep emotions within him when he first heard it, and he longed to hear those words in his own life. Recognizing this desire, I decided to make his birthday special that year. I ordered a medal online and crafted a certificate with the line from the movie. He was in awe.

I started saying those words to him almost every day to recognize what an incredible husband he is. It became clear that when I acknowledged and celebrated his efforts, our marriage flourished.

I often tell my clients the story of the woman whose husband folded the laundry. In one scenario, he folds the laundry, but it's done "wrong." She criticizes and accuses him. He doesn't fold the laundry again.

In the other scenario, she sees the clothes folded differently than she likes, but she praises God that she has a thoughtful husband who folds the laundry for her. She thanks him genuinely. The husband feels like a champion and is willing to fold the laundry again and again.

Our words and actions have the power to shape our relationships. Our husbands are drawn to places where they feel valued and appreciated. Let us strive to create an atmosphere where they feel like the champions of our hearts every day.

Heavenly Father, thank You that You are King of kings and Lord of lords. *You are the King of our hearts. Would You help this appreciation we have for You overflow in our marriage? I thank You for my husband and the ways he loves me and sacrifices for our family. Would You heal any hurt that has built up in our marriage and has made him feel undervalued? Would You heal any hurt in my heart? Let us both do as much as we can to show our appreciation for each other.*

I desire to be a wife who helps my husband feel like he can fly. Let me look out for the littlest of things he does today and thank him and recognize his efforts with sincerity. I repent for any times I have criticized him or focused on his shortcomings. Instead, empower me to uplift and build him up with my words and attitudes. Let our home be filled with love, kindness, and gratitude. May we become champions of each other's hearts. May our affirmation and recognition create an atmosphere where our love can flourish and grow stronger with each passing day. Amen.

The more you call forth the good in your husband, the more good you will see.

love in action . . .

Together: Commit to celebrating each other's accomplishments. Replace criticism with affirmation.

For him: Consider a special gift to show your appreciation for all your husband does.

WEEK

50

GRUMBLE-FREE ZONE

A prayer for an uncomplaining heart

Do everything without complaining and arguing, so that no one can criticize you. Live clean, innocent lives as children of God, shining like bright lights.

PHILIPPIANS 2:14-15

It was a somber day to celebrate the life of my beloved grandmother. As we gathered for her funeral, my husband's family gave us a beautiful vase of flowers, which we placed in our car for the drive to the gathering to honor her memory.

Along the way, the bouquet toppled over, saturating our car with water. When we got home, Caleb assured me that he would clean up the car so I could rest after the emotionally draining day.

A few days later, we were heading to Nashville for a wedding. When I entered our SUV, a foul odor assaulted my senses. I lashed out at Caleb, convinced he hadn't cleaned the car thoroughly enough. He realized he had missed a hidden spot, and he tried various remedies to no avail.

As we drove, I was relentless in my complaints. Caleb prayed fervently to himself for my heart to cease its grumbling. The wedding was fun, but then came the ride home. That morning when I read God's Word, He clearly told me not to complain. So I was obedient.

"Oh, wow, it smells better," Caleb said. I just smiled and nodded. To my amazement, the smell gradually dissipated. It was as though God had intervened to remove the stench of complaint. As we practice a complaint-free attitude within our marriage, and instead are grateful and kind, we can transform the atmosphere and enhance our connection.

Dear heavenly Father, thank You for my husband. *I pray that he would turn any complaints into praises. Let him pour out his worries and burdens to You and serve me willingly out of the abundance of Your love. Give him strength to resist the temptation to complain. Let his words be a source of encouragement and positivity. Teach him to focus on the good in others and in our circumstances, even when challenges arise.*

I pray that I would also humbly serve my husband and care for his needs. Keep me from complaining. Instead, let me be honest with You about everything, and let praise flow from my lips. I pray that we would both act and speak without arguing or complaining. Forgive me for the times I've allowed complaints to sour the atmosphere.

May our marriage be a testimony of love, kindness, and grace. May the fragrance of our relationship be a pleasing aroma to those around us, reflecting Your love and goodness. Amen.

A heart filled with gratitude leaves little room for complaint.

love in action . . .

Together: Set aside time daily to say what you appreciate about each other.

For him: Practice a complaint-free attitude. Instead of voicing complaints, tell your husband what you are grateful for.

WEEK

51

TRUST HIS TIMING

A prayer for unexpected answers

All glory to God, who is able, through his mighty power at work within us, to accomplish infinitely more than we might ask or think.

EPHESIANS 3:20

As a young girl, I had a simple yet heartfelt prayer: to live across the street from my parents when I grew up. Little did I know that this ordinary childhood wish would one day become a testament to the incredible ways God answers our prayers.

Living in California, far from my family, I often felt the ache of separation. I longed to share in their daily lives and joys. During one visit with them, my dad, Caleb, and I were out for a walk when we received a call from my mom's friend, a real estate agent. She urged us to check out a house that would soon be listed. Coincidentally, we were just steps away from it.

Upon approaching the house, we were greeted by the current owners. We spent hours in their company, sharing stories and forming a connection. In the end, they offered to sell us their beautiful home without even listing it on the market.

The speed at which everything fell into place left us astounded. We are now the proud owners of a home located a mere four-tenths of a mile from my parents. My childhood prayer had been answered in a way I could have never imagined. God not only hears our prayers but also orchestrates events in the most unexpected ways to fulfill the desires of our hearts with His goodness.

Heavenly Father, I come before You with a heart of gratitude for the remarkable ways You answer our prayers. *You have a knack for turning the ordinary into the extraordinary, and I stand in awe of Your wisdom and love. Thank You for the dreams my husband and I have held close to our hearts. I trust that Your divine orchestration will guide our marriage and life. I praise You for Your unceasing care and provision.*

I pray for the desires of my husband's heart. I know that You hear his prayers. Let him never give up on praying and listening to You. Help him to trust You with all of the dreams and desires of his heart.

In moments when he doubts whether You hear his prayers or when the fulfillment of his desires seems distant, help him to remember Your faithfulness. Teach him to trust Your timing and Your unique way of bringing about answers to his petitions.

May our lives be a testimony to Your unfailing love, a reminder to others that You are a God who not only listens but also moves mountains. Amen.

God weaves the threads of our prayers into a beautiful masterpiece. Trust His timing, for He answers in unexpected ways.

love in action . . .

Together: Reflect on how God has answered prayers for a longtime desire. Thank Him for His faithfulness.

For him: Encourage your husband with reminders of how God has been faithful to answer prayers for the two of you.

WEEK

52

UNDIVIDED ATTENTION

A prayer for quality time together

For husbands, this means love your wives, just as Christ loved the church. He gave up his life for her.

EPHESIANS 5:25

We needed a pause. The demands of work, ministry, and everyday responsibilities had begun to overshadow quality time and affection in our marriage. We had been tirelessly working on our online ministry, and we sensed a growing need to just be husband and wife, away from the daily grind.

That's when the opportunity for a work trip to Punta Mita presented itself. It felt like a gift from heaven—a chance to escape to paradise and reconnect. After completing our work, we enjoyed being pampered, savored exquisite cuisine, and basked in the beauty of nature. We took lazy river rides and sunset strolls on the beach, and we witnessed baby turtles making their journey to the ocean, which all became cherished memories.

But it wasn't just the breathtaking setting; it was the uninterrupted time together that made the trip truly special. We talked about our dreams, reflected on God's faithfulness, and held each other close in our hammock "nest" by the beach. Those moments were a reminder that quality time and affection are gifts we can give each other every day.

Every marriage deserves moments of undivided attention and genuine affection. It might not always be in a tropical paradise, but it can be in the simplicity of a heartfelt conversation, a warm embrace, or shared laughter. In these moments, we strengthen the bonds of our marriage and show our love in tangible ways.

Heavenly Father, thank You that You always want to spend time with me. *Help my husband and me to always desire to spend time with You and invite You into every moment.*

Thank You for my husband. I pray that he would desire to spend even more time with me. I pray he would make room in his schedule and be intentional about being in my presence. I pray he would look me in the eye, care about what I'm saying, and actively listen. I pray he would show me affection and love.

Help us to delight in time together. Provide ways for us to get away and enjoy the beauty of Your creation. Thank You for the gift of quality time and affection. Help us to prioritize these moments, even in the midst of busy schedules. May we continue to nurture our connection and keep the flame of affection burning brightly. Amen.

**Every moment spent together is a treasure.
Cherish and nurture your love daily.**

love in action . . .

Together: Plan a date night or getaway to enjoy quality time together. Express your affection through words, acts of kindness, and physical touch.

For him: Make a point of connecting with your husband each day. Look him in the eye, actively listen, and show him affection.

Acknowledgments

To Jesus, the savior of my soul. No words can express how You've flipped and keep flipping my life upside right. God, You've held me in the palm of Your hand since I was born. Holy Spirit, You stay close to me, and I feel Your guidance. Thank You for giving me every good thing and being the glue of my marriage.

To the love of my life, Caleb. If my life were shown as a movie, my favorite parts would be the memories of looking into your eyes. From the moment we first talked, I saw something different there that I wanted more of. When I caught your gaze, it held a depth that drew me in, filling me with a sense of peace. Your eyes are like windows to my soul, and they unlock places in my heart that I didn't know were there. Through every triumph and trial, they remain constant, filled with an unwavering love and tenderness that touch the deepest parts of my being. Even in moments of pain and loss, your look of love is something I cherish beyond words. Your eyes, dear Caleb, reflect back to me a love I hadn't seen in myself and show me a man who is filled with positivity, integrity, kindness, and humility. This book is dedicated to the love that shines in your eyes and the way you light up my world.

To my children, Shiloh and Asher in heaven. Caleb and I long to hold you in our arms, but we know you are in safe hands. We love you, and we hope to honor you in how we help and love others. We can't wait to see you in heaven. Say hi to Jesus for us. To any future children God might bless us with: you will be our redemption story. We love you already.

To my parents, Ed and Susan Stack. You both are my heroes. The older I get, the more I appreciate you both and thank God for you. From the time I was a little girl you believed in me to be the best I could be. You spoke so much encouragement over my creativity in writing and drawing. You have sacrificed so much for me and for the dreams God has put on my heart. I'm forever grateful for the love, sacrifice, example, and generosity you have shown me every day of my life. I am so grateful God chose you to be my parents. Your hard work ethic and the way you pour your heart and soul into loving others is such an inspiration. The way you love and embrace Caleb and have helped our dreams come true is something I cherish always. I love you both so much.

To my in-laws, "Papa" John and "Momma" Kay. Your love for each other, the romance, the fun you continually cultivate show that love can last forever. Thank you for your support and encouragement in making this dream of ours come true. Caleb and I feel every prayer, and we are so thankful for all the ways that you are there for us in good and difficult times. You motivate us to see the best in each other and to fight for each other and remember that we can all come together in prayer to have peace no matter our circumstance.

To my grandma Maryann "Nanny" Miller, to Grandpa "Pappy" Bob Miller (now in heaven), and to my Aunt Cindy. You are the most generous, loving humans. You continually think of others before yourselves. No matter what you have, you look for ways it could bless others. Pappy wrote me a letter a week for almost ten years. His funny, caring way inspired me to write and to go after my dreams. Nanny and Cindy, you continually support and love us and make this world a much better place.

To my grandpa Bill Stack, and to my grandma Tris Stack and my Aunt Dee (both now in heaven). You continually spoke love and inspiration over me. You've taught me to trust God, and you believed in my ability as a writer from the time I was little and writing Christmas plays for the family. You cultivated so much fun, joy, and unconditional love.

To my sister, Cristina. I'm so proud of the amazing woman and mom you are. I'm so grateful for you. It's been a blessing to get to do this life together with you since I was two. Thanks for being my little sister and being by my side through all the ups and downs. To Daniel, my brother-in-law, and our nephews, Daxton and Kadan: we love you so much. You bring so much joy, laughter, and fun into our lives. I'm so proud of you, Daxton and Kadan. God has such amazing plans for your life! I'm praying already for your future wives!

To Caleb's grandma Marcia. Thank you for your constant and consistent love and words of encouragement. You are an inspiration for endurance and grace in our lives. You have shown us how to overcome and to trust God in every season. We are grateful for you.

To Caleb's brothers, Matt and Jesse. Thanks for being great brothers to Caleb and me! You guys are such a gift in my life. And to Alicia, my sister-in-law, and our niece and nephew, Shirah and Josiah: I am so thankful for each of you, and I appreciate the love and encouragement you always show me. Shirah and Josiah, I'm praying for your future husband and future wife. God has such amazing plans for you!

To Kara Leonino, Donna Berg, Sarah Atkinson, and the team at Tyndale House Publishers. Thank you for believing in us, for investing in our dreams, and for helping us share our story with the world. Thank you for your intentional feedback and your kindness, and for crying with us, laughing with us, and pushing us to make this book the best it can be.

To Andrea Heinecke, Alex Field, and The Bindery Agency. Working with you has allowed us to dream bigger and make a lifelong dream become a reality. We appreciate you for believing in us and for being our advocates throughout this process.

To my friends, family, and mentors. You are so valued and appreciated. I couldn't have done this project without you. We see you, and we love you so much. Thank you for believing in us.

To our Cultivate Relationship, *Wholehearted Love*, and Love Launchpad women and men, and to all those we have the huge honor of mentoring. Your courage, love, kindness, and growth are so inspiring. We love you and believe in you. We are so proud of you, and we know God is in the midst of redeeming everything in your life!

To our online community. You are loved beyond measure! God has an amazing plan for your life, and we hope this book inspires you to realize that you are not forgotten. The pain and heartbreak you have experienced are not the end of the story. God has so much in store for you! Thank you for your encouragement and support!

About the Author

Stefanie Rouse and her husband, Caleb, are dynamic relationship mentors and digital creators passionately guiding singles and couples toward fulfilling and resilient relationships anchored in faith. With their master's degrees in marriage and family therapy with an emphasis in theology (Stefanie) and in education (Caleb), they offer tailored courses, mentorship, and guidance. These are all rooted in prayer and backed by training in psychology and biblical counseling, encouragement from Christ, and practical strategies for love that lasts. Engaging an audience across multiple social media platforms, Stefanie and Caleb provide daily insights into the transformative power of Jesus' love for all relationship stages. Their vision is a world where we learn to love each other out of God's abundance of love, leading to impactful and joyous relationships.